Decorative
PAINTED
FURNITURE

Decorative
PAINTED
FURNITURE

MAGGIE PHILO

MEREHURST

Published in 1996 by Merehurst Limited
Ferry House, 51–57 Lacy Road, Putney, London SW15 1PR

ISBN 1 85391 501 7

A catalogue record for this book is available from
the British Library.

Edited by **Heather Dewhurst**
Designed by **Maggie Aldred**
Photography by **Jon Bouchier** (pp. 8–9, 11, 27, 30, 32–34,
36–38, 40, 42–44, 46–48, 50–52, 54–56, 58, 60–62, 64–66, 68–72,
74–76, 78, 80–84 and 86–87) and **Anna Hodgson** (pp. 1, 7,
28–29, 31, 35, 39, 41, 45, 49, 53, 57, 59, 63, 67, 73, 77, 79 and 85)
Styling by **Clare Louise Hunt** (pp. 1, 7, 28–29, 31, 35, 39, 41, 45,
49, 53, 57, 59, 63, 67, 73, 77, 79 and 85)
Illustrations by King & King Design Associates

Typesetting by Servis Filmsetting Ltd
Colour separation by P&W Graphics, Singapore
Printed in Italy by L.E.G.O. S.p.a.

Contents

Introduction 6

E Q U I P M E N T A N D M A T E R I A L S 8

P A I N T I N G T E C H N I Q U E S 18

P R O J E C T S 28

Antiqued kitchen cupboard 30

Limed picture frame 34

Crackle-glazed chair 37

Handpainted chest 40

Découpaged bathroom cabinet 43

Handprinted blanket box 47

Chequered table and chair 51

Scumble-glazed table 55

Craquelure lamp base 58

Stencilled bedside chest 62

Gilded mirror frame 66

Verdigris metal table 71

Lined clock cupboard 75

Lacquered butler's tray 78

Frottaged and stencilled screen 83

Templates 88

Suppliers 94

Index 94

Acknowledgements 96

Introduction

Having written three books on decoupage techniques, it was lovely to be asked to write a book on painting furniture. I have taught and used decorative techniques for painting furniture and walls for far longer than I have been practising découpage. In fact, I first tried my hand at découpage in order to teach it as one of many treatments for the decoration of furniture.

Painting furniture is certainly not a new idea and it has been practised and admired for literally thousands of years. After a period of decline during this century, it is now enjoying enormous popularity, both as a fashionable decorating style and as a satisfying craft. I believe this is due partly as a result of the mass production of furniture, which all looks the same. Not many people can afford to have custom-built furniture nowadays, and painting it is a way of creating an individual style.

When decorating furniture we can draw upon the influences of oriental laquerwork and the exquisite decoration on ornate pieces of the 17th and 18th centuries. Scandinavian and American folk or country designs are other popular influences today and their often simple patterns and designs make them a good choice of style for the novice decorator.

The chances are that you will already have your fair share of furniture that needs to be decorated. If this is not the case, however, you will find no shortage of suitable items to buy. Many of the pieces decorated in this book were new, but they were not expensive. Every item I used cost less than £100, and most were less than half that. Similar pieces can be bought from home furnishing and DIY stores, or from mail order suppliers that produce furniture especially to be decorated. Look in the classified advertisement section in the back of home interest and craft magazines and you will find many such companies. Perhaps the most rewarding sources of furniture for decoration are junk shops and car boot sales, where pieces can be bought very cheaply indeed, while those that are rescued from a skip cost nothing. The condition of this furniture does not really matter as chips, dents and scratches can either be lost beneath layers of filler and paint, or used to advantage to add to the aged look that is so fashionable today.

Before decorating a piece of furniture, try out techniques and colours by painting samples on to pieces of wood, medium density fibreboard (MDF) or even cardboard. My local timber yard allows me to have off-cuts of floorboards for free and I am regularly collecting a laundry bag full to experiment with!

I have used, wherever possible, water-based eco-friendly products throughout this book. The main exception is the use of shellac, which is spirit based. There have been some tremendous advances recently in creating water-based products to replace solvent-based ones, and this trend is continuing with more and more appearing on the market. This is not only very good news for the environment, but also for the user, with brushes simply being washed out with water and no unpleasant fumes and odours to endure.

There was only room for 15 projects in this book and, with the overwhelming choice of furniture available, not to mention the countless ways and colours to decorate it, it was very hard to choose. I hope the final choice reflects the variety in style and colour that you can achieve with paint.

Equipment and Materials

With so many different decorating techniques covered in the projects section, there is rather a daunting array of materials shown. Most are water based, inexpensive and can be found easily in art and craft shops or DIY stores. Other more specialist items can be bought by mail order if you are unable to find them locally.

Basic equipment

PAINT

This is by far the most important ingredient and a successful result is very much dependent on your choice of paint and colour. The furniture in this book was decorated with standard emulsion paint, chalky textured traditional paint or with pure powder pigment mixed with these paints and other mediums. In addition, artist's acrylic colours have been used for some of the surface decoration. All are water based and quick drying.

Emulsion Paint This is easily found, fairly inexpensive and comes in an enormous range of colours with a choice of matt or satin finish. It is a tough plastic paint which is waterproof when dry. Some manufacturers now produce a good range of historic colours to meet the current trend in creating a period look. You can sometimes find 250ml (8fl oz) tester pots which are very economical when painting a small item. Emulsion paint can be thinned with water to make a wash and it can be tinted with acrylic paints, universal stainers or powder pigments to create your own colours.

Traditional Paint A number of so-called traditional paints have recently appeared on the market. These use natural pigments, rather than the synthetic ones that are used to make emulsion paint. They also contain chalk, a traditional ingredient used in paint-making and dry to a completely matt finish that appears considerably lighter than the colour in the pot. Most of these paints include modern binders and, although they have the feel and look of those used in the past, they have the advantage of a greater degree of durability. However, they are easily marked and painted surfaces need protecting with wax or varnish. Applying varnish and waxes over traditional paints will darken them and take away their chalky appearance. Traditional paints are a little more expensive than standard emulsion paint but are definitely my preferred choice. Not only do the colours have a wonderful softness and subtlety, but the paint is not skin forming

There are many different paints you can use to decorate furniture, ranging from emulsion and traditional paints, to artist's colours. You can also mix pure powder pigment with paints to extend the colour range.

and handles very well when creating a distressed finish. These paints are very quick drying and are usually recoatable within about half an hour. They can be thinned with water and tinted in the same way as emulsion paint.

Powdered Pigments and Rottenstone Natural earth and mineral pigments in powder form can be mixed with other paint colours, acrylic and PVA mediums, and wax. They are available in a wonderful range of colours from good art and specialist decorating shops. Rottenstone is a finely ground greyish-brown limestone powder. It is usually used for polishing but is good for giving an aged appearance and can be used in the same way as powder pigment.

Artist's Acrylic Paint This paint is very quick drying and durable. Its concentrated colour makes it ideal for many types of surface decoration, including stencilling, printing and the painting of flowers and other ornament. It is sold in a good range of colours in tubes or jars. A number of art and craft shops also sell small pots of craft paint. This usually contains concentrated acrylic colour in rather softer shades and is equally suitable.

PRIMERS

Acrylic Primer This quick-drying primer is generally used for sealing wood, but some makes of acrylic primer are also suitable for metal, masonry and other materials. It is usually white in colour.

Oil-based Primer This is a slow-drying durable primer which is useful for surfaces that do not easily accept or grip acrylic primers. This includes some metal and plastic surfaces. I never find it necessary to use oil-based primer on wooden furniture. You will need to work in a well-ventilated room when using oil paint because of the fumes, which can be quite strong. Always clean brushes with white spirit.

Rust-inhibiting Primer This paint can be either slow drying and oil based, or quick drying and spirit based. It is absolutely essential to use it before applying water-based paint to metal that shows signs of, or is likely to, rust. It is not usually necessary to use it on new galvanized metal or tin. Work in a well-ventilated room when using this paint and clean brushes according to the manufacturer's instructions.

BRUSHES

Household Paint Brushes Use these brushes for applying emulsion or traditional paints and primers. You will find a 2.5cm (1in), 4cm (1½in) and 5cm (2in) brush the most useful sizes.

Use household paint brushes for applying emulsion and traditional paints, flat hog's-hair brushes for applying varnish, and artist's brushes for detailed work. Specialist decorating brushes are available for stencilling, lining and dusting.

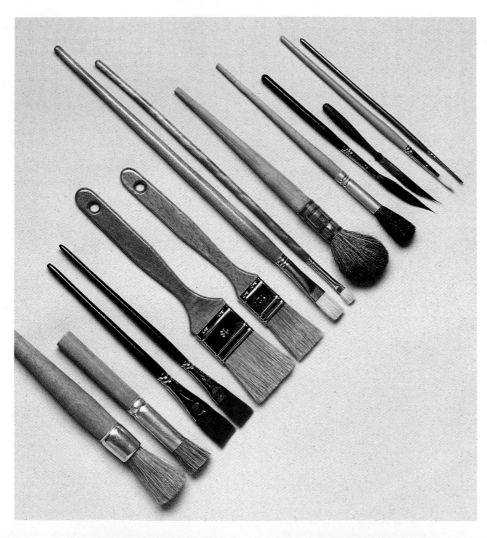

Varnish Brushes Flat hog's-hair varnish brushes can be obtained from specialist decorating shops and some art shops. They are particularly nice to use for brushing on a thin layer of acrylic varnish but are not essential and household brushes can be used instead. I also use these brushes for applying thin coats of colourwashes and glazes.

Artist's Brushes A variety of artist's brushes are needed for different applications and all are obtainable from art and craft shops. *Fine pointed brushes* are required for painting finely detailed designs. These are made from sable which is best for watercolour, or synthetic hair which is best for acrylic. It is important to wash brushes out immediately after use with acrylic paint as, once dry, they cannot be cleaned. *Flat-haired synthetic brushes* are fairly expensive, but they are very good for applying two-part crackle varnish and acrylic goldsize as they are very soft and leave no brush marks on the surface. A 2cm (¾in) brush is a good choice of size for most purposes, but a 2.5cm (1in) brush is worth having if you can afford it. *Hog fitches* are a good all-purpose brush. They are generally used for oil painting and can be round, flat or dome shaped. Painting narrow bands of colour, applying glue, waxes and gilt cream, touching up paint and tamping down metal leaf, are among the many uses for these brushes.

Specialist Decorating Brushes I have kept these to a minimum and all can be obtained from specialist decorating suppliers. *Stencil brushes* are additionally available from many art, craft and DIY shops. They are usually made from hog's hair and are round and firm-bristled. When stencilling with acrylic paint, you will need to choose brushes that have a little give in the bristle rather than the very firm variety. Stencil brushes can also be used to stipple paint in small areas and to spatter paint. *Sword liners* are long-haired, soft brushes that are tapered and angled. They are capable of producing many widths of line simply by varying the pressure applied to the brushstroke. *Soft-haired mops* are round brushes which are used in gilding to dust bronzing

You can achieve very different finishes by using traditional paint on its own (bottom left), with antique yellowing wax (top left), with walnut brown wax (top right), or with varnish (bottom right).

powder on to goldsize. They can be bought inexpensively, but you could use a soft squirrel paint brush from an art shop instead.

ABRASIVES

Sandpaper and Finishing Paper Sandpaper comes in a range from fine to coarse and is used to prepare a surface for decoration, to distress paint and to smooth paints and varnishes. It is readily available in DIY stores. Less easily found, but worth looking out for, are silicone carbide finishing papers. They are obtainable in much finer grades and I like to use them to give a smooth finish to varnish and to distress a painted surface without scratching it. Trade decorating suppliers generally stock finishing paper. A sanding block is useful for wrapping the papers around when working on a flat surface.

Wire Wool Wire wool also ranges from fine to coarse. It can be used for rubbing down furniture to prepare it

for decoration but, in this book, I have used it for distressing the painted surface. I have used either 00 or 0000 grade, which are both fine grades.

Wire Brushes These are used to open up the grain on wood before liming and to remove flaking paint and rust. Wire brushes are inexpensive and readily available in hardware and DIY shops.

WAXES

Furniture waxes have been used throughout the book and good ranges are available from specialist decorating shops and suppliers to the wood turning and antique restoration trades.

Clear Waxes Clear furniture wax is an effective resist (that is, it creates a block, preventing paint from reaching a surface) when creating an aged appearance to furniture. Use it over paint or wood where you don't want a colour to adhere to, such as areas of wear. Clear liquid

To apply liming wax to a surface, dip wire wool in liming wax then rub it gently over the surface. This will tone down the colour of the paint.

widely used for furniture restoration and french polishing and is used as a stainer and sealant for many of the projects in this book. You can buy it from specialist decorating and DIY shops, and suppliers to the wood turning and antique restoration trades. Shellac comes in a variety of grades and colours and is sold, rather confusingly, under many different names. Use clear shellac sanding sealer, white french polish and white button polish for sealing wood, paper and paint. Use brown french polish or garnet polish for staining and ageing in addition to sealing. French enamel varnish is transparent shellac with added dye and is good for ageing and sealing wood. You should use methylated spirit to clean brushes used for applying shellac; methylated spirit is also used to thin shellac solutions.

Two-part Crackle Varnish This consists of a slow-drying oil-based varnish and a quick-drying water-soluble varnish. The water-soluble varnish is brushed over a layer of very slightly tacky oil-based varnish and a short time later a cracked porcelain effect occurs due to the difference in drying times. This becomes clearly visible when you rub artist's oil colour over the surface as it gets caught in the cracks. Oil-based goldsize and gum arabic water can be used to achieve this effect, but it is less reliable than commercially produced packs. Brushes used for the oil-based varnish need to be cleaned with white spirit.

Water-based Varnish Water-based acrylic varnishes are now widely available in gloss, satin or matt finishes. A dead flat varnish is also available but less easily found. This is very flat, whereas matt varnish usually has a slight sheen. Acrylic varnishes are milky in appearance, but dry to a clear finish and are non-yellowing. However, the matt and dead flat versions contain chalk which gives them a cloudy appearance when a number of coats are applied. This makes them unsuitable to use for the many layers that découpage requires. These finishes are also softer and less durable than satin or gloss varnish. Some brands of acrylic varnish contain polyurethane for extra toughness. Water-based varnish is usually dry to

wax is particularly good for this and is obtainable from specialist suppliers. Clear wax is also used as a finishing wax over paint or matt varnish; it can be coloured with rottenstone and other pigments.

Coloured Waxes A large variety of brown or antiquing furniture waxes are obtainable; these are used for staining wood. Walnut shades are good for ageing all colours of paint but the antiquing waxes are generally yellowing and should be avoided on blue paint. However, they do give a wonderful glow to many shades of yellow and green paint.

Liming Wax Liming wax is a mix of clear wax and white pigment and it is used to give a pickled lime effect to wood. It can also be used as a finishing wax.

VARNISHES

Shellac Shellac is the naturally occurring resin of the lac beetle and it is mixed with methylated spirit to form a quick-drying varnish. This traditional product is

the touch in about 20 minutes and recoatable after two hours. It is now the only varnish I use to protect furniture, unless I have used a craquelure technique.

Oil-based Varnish This is a slow-drying varnish, available in polyurethane or alkyd formulas. It is usually recoatable after about eight hours or the following day and, although it is generally more durable and heatproof that water-based varnish, it does yellow with time. It is necessary to use an oil-based varnish to seal water-soluble crackle varnish. Work in a well-ventilated room and clean brushes with white spirit.

GLAZES AND MEDIUMS

Crackle Glaze This is a water-soluble glaze that is applied as a sandwich between two layers of paint or between wood and paint. It dries clear in about half an hour, and causes the paint that is applied over the dry glaze to crack, giving the appearance of peeling paint. Crackle glaze is available from specialist decorating suppliers and some art, craft and DIY shops.

Acrylic Scumble This is a fairly slow-drying water-based transparent glaze medium to which colour is added. It is used for creating transparent textured effects such as stippling, sponging and dragging. The marks that you make with brushes, sponges and other tools are held by the consistency of the glaze. It is not necessary to add water but, if you do, be careful not to overdo it or it will lose its texturing properties. Acrylic scumble can be bought from specialist decorating suppliers and a few art and DIY shops.

PVA and Acrylic Mediums These water-based mediums are coloured white but dry transparent. A wide range is available from art, craft and DIY shops. PVA can be used as a glue or varnish and, when thinned with water, as a paint medium or binder. It can also be mixed with acrylic, gouache, universal stainers or powder pigment to make paints and washes. Artist's acrylic mediums are very useful for extending acrylic paints and for mixing with pure powder pigment to make concentrated acrylic colour.

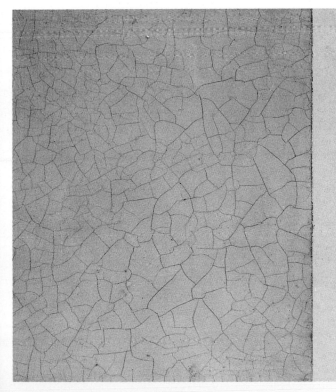 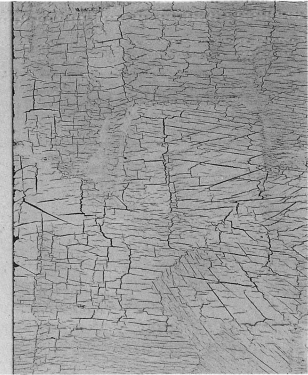

Using two-part crackle varnish produces fine cracks, giving the effect of cracked porcelain (left), while using crackle glaze causes the paint applied over the top to crack, giving the appearance of peeling paint (right).

Transfer metal leaf is a good substitute for real gold and silver. You can also use bronzing powder and gilt creams which have more lustre than gold paint.

SOLVENTS

Water is the most commonly used solvent in this book, but white spirit and methylated spirit are also used sparingly. They are both widely available from hardware and DIY stores.

White Spirit White spirit is used to thin oil-based paints and varnishes and to remove them from brushes and other surfaces. It can be very unkind to skin, so if you have sensitive skin, protect your hands with rubber gloves or a barrier cream available from a chemist.

Methylated Spirit Methylated spirit is used as a solvent for emulsion paint when creating a distressed effect and it can be used on wet or dry paint. It is also used as a solvent, thinner and brush cleaner for shellac and french enamel varnish. Methylated spirit is good for de-greasing and removing some lacquers from furniture prior to decoration. Use a fine-grade wire wool for this purpose.

METAL LEAF, POWDER, CREAM AND SIZE

Transfer Metal Leaf Bronze, aluminium and copper leaf are inexpensive and a good substitute for real gold and silver when adding decorative touches to furniture. Transfer leaf, which is sold in packs of 25 sheets, is available from specialist suppliers and good art shops. Each sheet consists of very finely beaten metal backed with waxed paper. The metal is transferred from the paper on to tacky size. Metal leaf tarnishes in time, so it needs to be sealed with shellac or varnish.

Bronzing Powder Bronzing powders are finely ground metallic powders made from bronze, aluminium and copper. They are dusted on to a tacky size, and look less shiny than metal leaf, but have more lustre than gold paint. They can also be mixed with mediums to make a metallic paint. Bronzing powders are available in a wide range of shades from specialist suppliers and art shops.

Acrylic Goldsize This is a water-based size that appears milky but turns transparent within about 15 to

GLUES AND FILLERS

Glues *Wood glue* is available in a strong PVA formula and is readily available in most good DIY stores. You will need this to mend broken pieces of furniture and for gluing on wooden mouldings. *Paper glue* can be either PVA or a paste glue available from stationers and art shops. It is needed for the découpage projects (see pp.43 and 75).

Wood Filler There are many types of wood filler available from DIY shops and you will need to follow the specific manufacturer's instructions. I like to use the water-based varieties that are now available and are simple to use.

20 minutes of brushing it on to a surface. It is then ready to accept metal leaf and powder.

Gilt Creams These are a mix of bronzing powders and wax and are available in a number of shades from art and specialist decorating shops. They can be applied with a firm brush or a finger.

STENCIL AND PATTERN-MAKING EQUIPMENT

Stencil Making *Stencil film* is made from transparent polyester sheeting, which is very flexible and durable. A stencil design can be traced directly on to the film with a pencil. It is available from specialist stencil suppliers. Thinner polyester sheets are available from graphic art shops; these are fine if the stencil is not to be used repeatedly. *Acetate* is a good alternative, but more prone to tearing. You will need to trace the design on the acetate with a suitable marking pen.

Tracing and Transfer Paper *Tracing paper* is needed for tracing a design to be transferred on to a piece of furniture. *Transfer paper* is coated with a chalky film and is coloured red, blue, black and white. It is placed between the design to be transferred and the surface to be decorated. The outline is then transferred by tracing over it with a pen or pencil.

Drawing Instruments A *ruler* is an essential piece of equipment, both for measuring and marking out a design. I find a 45cm (18in) centring ruler, from a graphic art supplier, a very useful piece of equipment. A *straight edge* is needed for some of the projects. A *set square* is also useful, but a frame, book or other rectangular object can be used instead. A *water-soluble pencil* is useful for marking out designs that can be wiped off later.

CUTTING EQUIPMENT

A *scalpel knife* is needed for cutting stencils, cardboard templates and découpage cut-outs. This is available from art and craft shops. A pair of sharp *manicure scissors* is also needed to cut out paper for découpage. A *cutting mat* or a piece of thick cardboard is needed to protect your work surface when using a scalpel knife. A self-healing cutting mat, available from art and craft shops, is particularly good and lasts many years.

SUNDRIES

Masking tape can often be too sticky and, when you remove it from a surface, it can sometimes take a layer of paint with it, especially if it has been left in place for several days or weeks. To avoid this, de-tack the tape by pressing it first against cotton cloth. *Flexible masking tape* can now be found in many DIY shops and is very useful for masking around curved surfaces. *Mutton cloth* or stockinet, available from DIY shops, is used for polishing and mopping up. It can also be used to create texture on a painted surface that resembles stippling and eliminates brush marks. A *clean lint-free rag* is handy for mopping up but supplies in our house are not endless. I couldn't be without *kitchen paper*. I use it for applying shellacs and polishes, for rubbing in and wiping off paint, mopping up spills and buffing waxes. A *household sponge* is needed to clean off excess glue for the découpage process. I collect yoghurt pots, margarine tubs and other plastic food packaging to use as *paint mixing pots* and *trays*, and I use disposable paper palettes from art shops for mixing acrylic colours.

Transfer a design on to a piece of furniture by tracing it over transfer paper that you have taped on to the piece.

Painting Techniques

Most of the furniture that has been painted for this book has had some sort of ageing technique applied. This is a very forgiving decorating style as little lumps, wobbly lines and other minor imperfections can either enhance a handpainted look and add to the impression of age, or be lost beneath layers of antiquing glazes and wax.

Basic techniques

MANY OF THE TECHNIQUES USED IN THIS BOOK ARE described in detail within the project that they are used. This section includes more general basic techniques and additional advice.

PREPARATION

New Wood Most new wood needs to be primed with either shellac or acrylic primer. Shellac, being transparent, is good if you want to retain the natural appearance of the wood, for instance if you are distressing a piece of furniture so that some of the wood is revealed beneath the paint. First, lightly sand the surface with a medium-grade sandpaper, then carefully brush on a coat of shellac sanding sealer.

Acrylic primer is solvent-free and more pleasant to use than shellac sanding sealer. I use this when a surface is going to be entirely painted. After you have brushed on the primer and left it to dry, lightly sand the surface with a medium-grade sandpaper. Smaller items made from good-quality wood without knots often do not need priming.

Old Wood Previously painted and varnished furniture needs to be thoroughly cleaned with detergent and water. When it is dry, rub it down with a coarse- or medium-grade sandpaper to remove all loose and flaking paint and provide a key to the surface. Highly lacquered surfaces will need a good deal of sanding with coarse sandpaper. If necessary, fill holes and cracks with a wood filler then sand the filled areas until they are smooth and level with the rest of the surface. It is then ready for painting in the colour of your choice. Previously polished wood will need to be rubbed down with 00 grade wire wool dipped in methylated spirit to remove the polish, then sanded with a medium-grade sandpaper when it is dry.

MDF Medium density fibreboard, or MDF, is rather like a very dense and finely textured chipboard. It is easily machined and less expensive than wood. Good-quality MDF needs no preparation at all and, not suprisingly, many companies are now producing MDF furniture.

Whiteboard This can be painted if you first rub it down with a coarse-grade sandpaper, then paint it with oil-based primer. Some brands of acrylic primer are suitable, but you will need to experiment. If you can scratch the primer off the surface with your fingernail, then you know it is not suitable.

Metal New galvanized metal and tin without any traces of rust must first be cleaned with detergent and water, then painted with an oil-based or acrylic metal primer.

To prepare old wood for decoration, rub it down with coarse-grade sandpaper wrapped around a sanding block. This removes all loose and flaking paint.

Old and rusting metal, or metal that is liable to rust, must be treated with a rust-inhibiting metal primer. After cleaning thoroughly, remove all loose and flaking rust with a coarse-grade sandpaper. Then paint on two coats of primer following the manufacturer's instructions. If the metal is not treated in this way, rust marks will soon appear on the painted surface.

PAINTING

Choosing Colours Choosing a colour can be agonising! There is so much choice, and one colour might look just as good as another one, or will it? Most people tend to play safe and choose a rather neutral colour. While this is rather unadventurous, there is something to be said for painting furniture this way because it will fit in with many different rooms and colour schemes. Of course, when deciding on a colour, reference must be made to walls and furnishings in the room in which you intend the decorated furniture to go. However, I do hope this book will inspire you to experiment with colour and explore the possibilities of different combinations.

You will find that natural earth pigments, which are wonderfully warm and soft colours, are very easy to live with and extremely adaptable. These colours have been used in paint-making for centuries; they are literally made of finely ground earth and are very inexpensive. With the addition of white they make very pretty pastel shades. Cooler shades of green and blue can be chosen from beautiful mineral colours.

Although there are no rules about colour choice, looking at magazines and books on interior decoration can be a helpful starting point. It will give you an idea of traditional colour combinations and which colours look good together. For example, you will frequently see country furniture painted in shades of blue and green with a hint of red ochre showing through where the paint has worn; you will probably notice that the centre of door panels are generally lighter than the surrounds, and so on.

When choosing more than one overall colour with perhaps panels and borders being picked out in other shades, you will find that using different tones of the

Metallic surfaces should be primed with an oil-based or acrylic metal primer before being decorated.

same colour gives subtlety and unity to a decorative theme. Choosing contrasting colours makes more of a statement, which can be striking and add interest, but be careful when using two colours of equal intensity as they can fight against each other.

COLOUR MIXING

Paint does come in the most enormous range of colours, but you will find it useful if you can learn some simple lessons about colour mixing and how to make subtle changes to colours.

Most people understand that you can lighten a colour by adding white and darken or dull a colour by adding black. However, there are other more subtle and interesting alternatives to black. Raw umber is a neutral shade of greyish-brown, a bit like the colour of mud. This can be added to any colour, even white, to tone it down and it immediately gives an old appearance to paint.

Complementary colours are colours that appear opposite each other in a colour wheel; very simply, red is opposite to green, yellow to purple and blue to orange. If complementary colours are mixed in equal quantities they become dark grey and muddy, but a touch of one to the other will darken and tone it down without making the colour look dead, in the way that black can. An exception, however, is blue which takes the addition of black well.

There are no rules about which colours should or should not be mixed together. Many unlikely combinations can produce very interesting shades. It is a question of experimenting and developing an eye for colour. In time you will find it much easier to look at a colour and know how it will change by adding another colour.

Mixing Pigment with Paint and Paint Mediums

Using powdered pigment is a satisfying and economical way of obtaining a wide range of colours. It is necessary to have a medium to bind the pigment and this can be done by mixing pigment with white and other coloured paint as well as glazes and PVA and acrylic mediums. If you are mixing pigment with emulsion or traditional paint, add the powder to a small amount of paint and a little water and mix it together well. Then add more paint until you have the required shade. A large amount of added pigment will make the paint very thick and you will need to thin it with water. Sometimes, although the paint looks thoroughly well mixed in a pot, it looks less so when painted on to a surface. This unevenness of colour adds to its charm and gives a more authentic appearance of age. For darker or more intense shades, you can mix pigment with PVA medium or glue and water, or with artist's acrylic medium. It does make a rather plastic paint without texture, but it is good for painting designs and adding detail and, when diluted, it is good for colourwashing and glazing. When using acrylic scumble glaze for a textured effect, you will only need to add a small amount of pigment and it is not necessary to add water. Artist's acrylic colours and universal stainers can be used in place of powdered pigment in any of these ways and all these pigments and mediums are compatible with each other, so enjoy experimenting. When mixing pigment with paint, always work in a room that is well-ventilated and take care not to inhale the pigment powder as it can be toxic.

Yellow ochre	Ultramarine blue
Raw sienna	Prussian blue
Burnt sienna	Cerulean blue
Red ochre	Viridian green
Venetian red	Oxide of chromium
Cadmium red	Raw umber
Alizarin crimson	Burnt umber

On the left is a suggested selection of useful acrylic pigments you can buy for making your own colours.

Create a variety of colours (right) by mixing them with their complementary colour, raw umber, black and then white, as in the first three horizontal rows. The last two horizontal rows show different combinations of blues, yellows and reds.

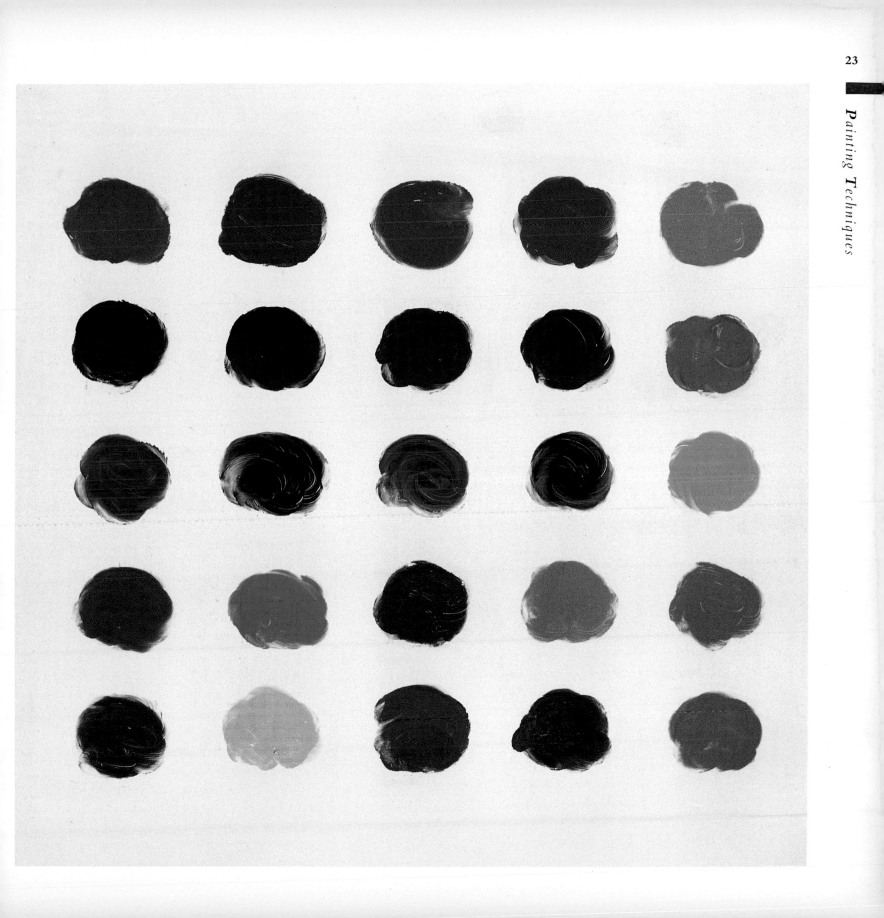

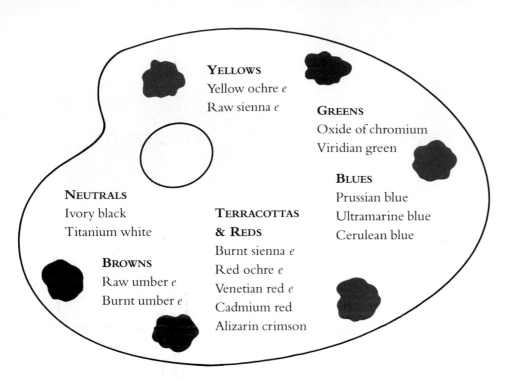

YELLOWS
Yellow ochre *e*
Raw sienna *e*

GREENS
Oxide of chromium
Viridian green

BLUES
Prussian blue
Ultramarine blue
Cerulean blue

NEUTRALS
Ivory black
Titanium white

**TERRACOTTAS
& REDS**
Burnt sienna *e*
Red ochre *e*
Venetian red *e*
Cadmium red
Alizarin crimson

BROWNS
Raw umber *e*
Burnt umber *e*

*Above is a palette of
pigments you need to make
your own paint colours.*

*To mix powders or pigments with paint (below),
add a tablespoon at a time and mix in thoroughly
until you achieve the colour you desire.*

On the left is a suggested palette for buying either powder or acrylic pigment for making your own colours. You will find these colours useful for decorating furniture, but you do not need to buy them all. The letter '*e*' denotes an earth pigment. Those without are mineral pigments.

APPLYING PAINT
I have found when teaching students techniques in painting furniture that most will automatically paint in even, straight lines. While I would always recommend brushing with, rather than across, the grain on wood, it is not necessary to attempt uniformly even strokes; you can quite happily paint in a relaxed, more random way. Indeed, this will give more texture and character to the surface of the piece.

When painting furniture that does not have a grain, such as whiteboard or MDF, you can still give it a wood-like appearance by brushing in the direction the grain would go, if it were made of wood. When painting metal and smaller decorative items, I usually paint in a completely random way, cross-hatching my brush-strokes. This leaves brush marks going in all directions and creates a lovely texture that looks good when used with antiquing glazes.

SURFACE PATTERN
There are many different techniques for applying surface pattern. These include transferring a design, handpainting, printing, découpage, stencilling, painting on lines and borders, creating geometric patterns, adding moulded relief, and gilding, to name a few. All of these are covered in the actual projects in the book (see pp.30–87). Although some of the patterns used for these are included at the end of the book for your reference (see pp.88–93), you will most certainly want to find your own and experiment.

There are books that are published especially for designers and craftspeople to use which contain copyright-free designs. The range of subjects and patterns covered is simply enormous and there is a good selection of books with designs taken from historical sources.

Paint in straight lines following the grain of the wood (left) or apply paint randomly, cross-hatching your brushstrokes for a textured effect (right).

To create an aged effect on furniture (below), gently rub the painted surface of the piece with wire wool dipped in methylated spirit.

An address where they can be obtained is included in the suppliers list (see p.94).

You will find many ideas for designs in home interest and craft magazines, as well as books on interior decoration. I cut out all kinds of pictures that I find interesting and keep them in a folder. This not only includes pictures of painted furniture, but colour combinations and patterns used on a diverse range of subjects that I find interesting and appealing.

THE AGEING PROCESS

There are many ways of giving an aged appearance to a piece of furniture and these are carried out at different stages of the decorating process, some before a piece is painted, and some after.

Before Painting Before you begin painting new wood, you can make it look old by darkening it with brown shellac solution or staining it with a water-based wood dye, such as walnut brown. To further age it you can throw a bunch of keys at it so that the surface becomes dented.

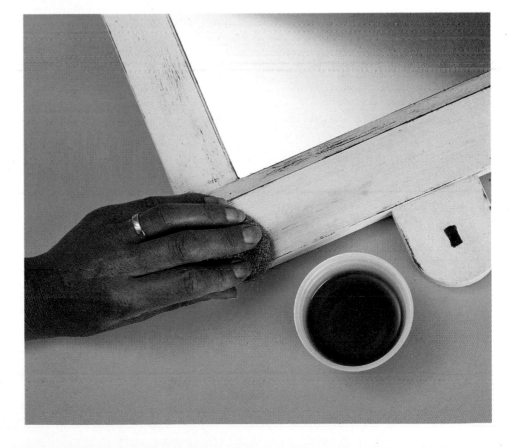

After Painting You can make the paint look worn after painting by distressing the surface with wire wool, sandpaper or finishing paper. These all have a slightly different effect on the paintwork and you can use a combination of these to achieve a result that you like. A wax resist can be applied in places of natural wear before painting, and this makes the rubbing-back process a bit easier, as does dipping wire wool in a little methylated spirit if you have decorated the piece with emulsion paint, or simply water if you have used traditional paints.

Antiquing Glaze This is another ageing device which, in effect, is like adding a layer of dirt to a piece! The antiquing glaze is mixed by adding raw umber pigment or rottenstone to a medium. There are recipes included in the Découpaged bathroom cabinet (see p.43) and Scumble-glazed table (see p.55) in this book, but you might like to experiment and invent your own glaze.

An antiquing glaze can be applied either directly on to paint or over varnish. You apply it with a brush or cloth, then wipe off the excess after a moment or two. When using it on a découpaged surface you need to seal it with two coats of varnish first, or it will spoil the paper surface. You can create the fly spots you sometimes see on old furniture, or a spattered effect, by dipping a stencil brush into the paint and flicking it on to the piece with a finger. Use a concentrated mix of raw umber or raw umber mixed with black.

Two-part Crackle Varnish This varnish can be used for a craquelure effect, creating the impression of cracked porcelain, but it is best to confine its use to smaller items at first. It looks particularly effective over light-coloured paint and on découpaged pieces. This technique is described fully in the Craquelure lamp base (see p.58).

Coloured Waxes These can be used on their own or in combination with the above varnishes and glazes to create an aged look to a painted surface, not only by colour, but also by the feel and subtle sheen they impart. The effect is quite unlike that of varnish. Wax is applied with a rag or kitchen paper and rubbed into the surface.

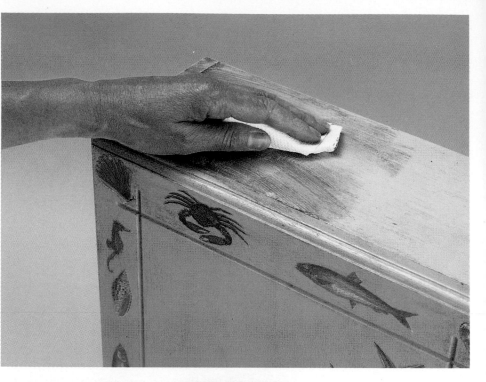

Apply antiquing glaze (above) with a brush or cloth, leave for a couple of minutes, then wipe off the excess with a piece of kitchen paper.

After varnishing a piece with two-part crackle varnish (left), mix raw umber artist's oil colour with a little white spirit and rub it into the cracks with kitchen paper.

FINISHING

Painted furniture normally needs protecting with either wax or varnish, or a combination of the two.

Satin Finish This is obtained by applying one or two coats of satin acrylic varnish over the final paint layer.

Matt Finish This is rather more subtle and, I think, nicer. It is achieved by brushing on one or two coats of matt or dead flat varnish. If you want a matt finish for découpage work, brush on two coats over the satin varnish that you will need to have used for a clear appearance.

Waxed Finish This can be applied either over paint or matt varnish and can be coloured or transparent. It has a less shiny appearance than satin varnish, and is usually the finish I choose. The varnish needs to be matt for the wax to adhere properly so, if you have used a satin varnish for the découpage process, you need to apply a coat of matt varnish before waxing. Alternatively, you can remove the shine from satin varnish by rubbing the surface with 0000 grade wire wool. With a large piece of furniture this is quite hard work! Apply the wax evenly with a rag or kitchen paper and leave it for about half an hour before buffing.

After Applying Crackle Varnish Crackle varnish is a water-soluble surface which needs to be sealed with an oil-based varnish, as instructed. If you would like a waxed surface, follow the same principles used above. Use a matt oil-based varnish, rather than a satin one, or rub the surface with 0000 grade wire wool to remove the shine.

Apply liming wax over a painted surface, leave for half an hour, then buff to a shine with a soft cloth.

Projects

The projects in this book vary in difficulty, with the easiest ones appearing at the beginning of the chapter and the most difficult ones towards the end. None, however, requires any drawing skills and you will be amazed at how easy it can be to transform a very ordinary piece of new furniture into a treasured 'old' one.

Antiqued kitchen cupboard

You will need:
- Detergent
- Water
- Cleaning cloth
- Coarse- and medium-grade sandpaper
- Wood filler
- Filling knife
- Clear liquid wax
- Small brush for applying wax
- Emulsion *or* traditional paint in 3 colours
- Paint brushes
- 00 grade wire wool
- Masking tape
- Kitchen paper
- Brown wax
- Soft cloth

We inherited this cupboard when we bought our house. It was hanging on, or rather off, the bathroom wall and it was promptly assigned to the attic where it stayed for many years, waiting for the right moment to be decorated. The paint was so badly chipped that it would have taken an enormous amount of time to fill it and put it in any sort of good order, so it seemed the ideal candidate for an aged and worn paint technique, using a wax resist over the existing areas of wear. If you want to use this technique on a new piece of furniture, you could repeat steps 2 and 3 twice in contrasting colours so that a second paint colour is revealed beneath the top coat. A set of keys bashed against the surface to create dent marks will further the illusion of age. The cupboard has a good shape and I felt it would look attractive decorating a kitchen wall. It is often nice to stencil or paint a design on to door panels, using perhaps a pair of cockerels or a folk art pattern. However, the

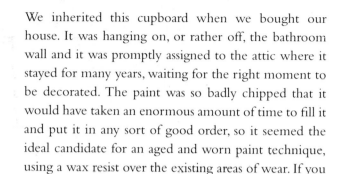

1 Clean the cupboard thoroughly by washing it with detergent and water, using a cloth. When it is dry, rub it down with a coarse-grade sandpaper to roughen the surface and remove all loose and flaking paint. Fill any large holes with wood filler. Brush on the liquid wax where you want to reveal the base coat, paying attention to the areas where the cupboard would naturally wear and the paint has chipped. You do not need to put it on the door panel as it is less likely to get worn there. Leave the wax to dry for about half an hour.

panels on this cupboard are very narrow, which restricts the choice of design I could use, and I chose instead to paint a contrasting band of colour on the surrounding edges to create interest. The same colour has also been used to paint the inside of the cupboard, which was then distressed without the use of wax resist; as you would not normally see this area, you may not want to go to the trouble of distressing it. Protect any paint on the inside with two coats of varnish rather than the wax used for the outside. When it comes to choosing a colour, there are no rules about whether you should put a light paint on top of a darker one, or a dark shade over a light one. Both work equally well, with the top colour being dominant, unless you are extremely energetic with wire wool and sandpaper and in the process remove most of it!

Having spent a considerable amount of time and effort carefully recreating its original worn look in a more interesting choice of colour, one of my daughters asked me if I was about to paint the cupboard for this book. She looked at me with absolute disbelief when I said that actually I just had!

2 Paint the cupboard with two coats of paint in the colours of your choice, allowing the first coat to dry thoroughly before applying the second. Start with the central door panel and, while this is drying, paint the sides and ends of the cupboard. Finally, paint the panel surrounds and then the inside of the cupboard if you wish to do so.

3 Using wire wool or medium-grade sandpaper, or a combination of the two, rub the painted surface until the colour beneath is revealed and you have achieved the desired antiqued effect. The paint should come off quite easily where the wax has been placed.

4 Stick masking tape inside the door panel, about 6mm (¼in) from the edge, to prevent any of the paint accidentally being applied to the panel, and paint with a contrasting colour. When the paint has dried, distress it lightly by rubbing with sandpaper.

5 Using a pad of kitchen paper, rub a brown or antique wax on to all the surfaces of the cupboard. Leave the wax to dry for about half an hour, then buff to a shine with a soft cloth.

Limed picture frame

You will need:
- Wire brush
- Dark-coloured emulsion
  or traditional paint
- Water
- Paint brush
- 2 soft cloths
- Liming wax
- 0000 grade wire wool
- Clear wax

The technique of liming has been used on furniture for centuries, originally to protect it from fungus and insects, then later as a decorative effect. The caustic properties of lime make it very unkind to skin, so nowadays we use a white pigment added to wax. It is possible to buy a water-based liming paste and, if you can obtain this, follow the same instructions as below but omit the clear wax from step 4 and apply it instead after you have removed the excess paste. Liming is a traditional way to treat oak, which is often very dark and has a marked and open grain. However, the technique can by used very effectively on pine if it is first brushed firmly with a wire brush and then colourwashed with paint or stained with wood dye. Although you will need to choose a dark colour to contrast with the white liming wax, the overall effect is soft and subtle. Liming is an ideal treatment for a picture frame as it allows you to choose a colour that will both enhance your picture and work with your room decoration. An inexpensive frame like I have used here can be ordered from any framing shop. You will need to specify that you want untreated pine.

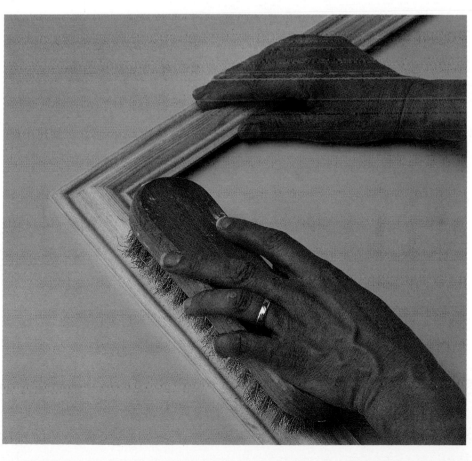

1 Open up the grain on the wood by brushing the surface of the picture frame firmly with a wire brush, always brushing in the direction of the grain. This could take about 15 minutes.

2 Brush a mixture of dark-coloured paint and water (1 part paint to 1 part water) on to the frame and leave it for a minute or so to sink in before wiping away the excess paint with a soft cloth.

3 When the paint has dried, apply the liming wax to the surface with wire wool. This will tone down the colour of the paint. Leave it for at least half an hour.

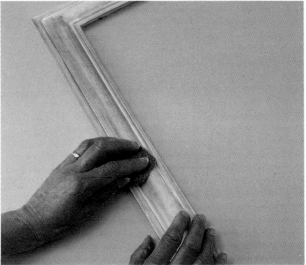

4 Using wire wool, rub the surface of the frame with clear wax to remove the excess liming wax. Leave the wax to dry for about half an hour and then buff the frame to a shine with a soft cloth.

Crackle-glazed chair

You will need:
- Emulsion *or* traditional paint in 2 contrasting shades
- Paint brushes
- Crackle glaze medium *or* gum arabic
- Medium-grade sandpaper
- Matt water-based varnish

It is easy to imagine this rustic Greek chair, with the worn paint cracked by the heat, being sat upon year after year by customers enjoying a glass or two of wine outside a sun-soaked taverna. I have used lovely Mediterranean blues for the chair, making my own colours by mixing cerulean blue and ultramarine powered pigments with white emulsion paint. Although a degree of confidence is required, the crackle technique used is very quick and simple and works by applying a cracking medium between two layers of paint. Good results are achieved with both ordinary emulsion paint and traditional paint, but there can be a variation in the extent of cracking between different brands of paint and even different colours from the same manufacturer. It is important that whichever paint you choose it is not too thick and has a good flow. It is a good idea to try out the technique first on a piece of scrap wood, experimenting with different thicknesses of both the crackle medium and the paint, until you find the combination that you are happy with.

The chair would make a cheerful addition to a garden room or conservatory, but if you plan this project for a not-so-sunny kitchen you may need to tone down the colouring. Colours that look terrific in southern climates do not always work so well in chillier ones with the different quality of light. Although, in this instance, I have used the crackle glaze together with the random application and distressing of the paint to give the impression of age, you can apply the glaze between two even layers of paint to create a purely decorative effect. You can create a very dramatic look by using a lacquer-red and black, or a subtler look by using two tones of the same colour.

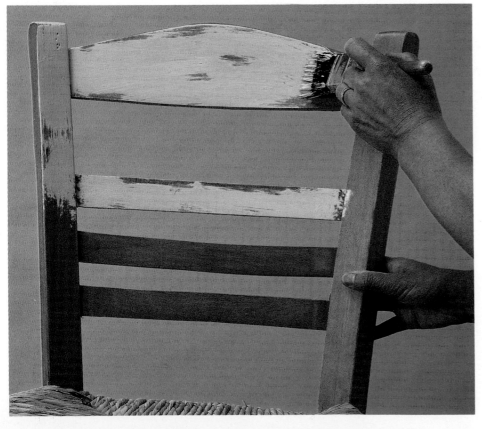

1 Paint the first paler colour on the chair rather patchily so that both bare wood and paint will be revealed beneath the cracks and add to the illusion of age. Leave to dry.

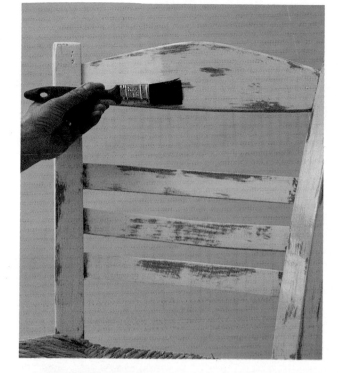

2 Brush on the crackle glaze or gum arabic. The thicker you
apply it, the larger the cracks will be. Leave the chair to dry
thoroughly before applying the next coat of paint. The medium
becomes more stable and easier to handle if you leave it for at
least four hours or overnight.

3 Brush on the second paint colour, again in a random
fashion, but covering most of the first colour. Try to work
quickly and confidently and do not go over an area you have
just painted more than once or you will reactivate the glaze and
the paint will start to skid and slide. Wait for the paint to dry
thoroughly then fill in any bits you have missed with more
paint. Allow to dry.

4 Using a medium-grade sandpaper wrapped around a
sanding block, rub back the paint to areas of natural wear.
This will reveal more of the base coat and soften out any hard
edges. Seal the paint with one or two coats of water-based
varnish, working quickly so as not to activate the crackle
medium. Allow the varnish to dry between coats. If you do not
seal the surface and the chair gets wet, the paint surface is likely
to be disturbed.

*H*andpainted chest

You will need:
- Deep red emulsion paint
- Paint brushes
- White emulsion paint
- Sandpaper
- Masking tape
- Pencil
- Tracing paper
- Transfer paper
- Fine-pointed artist's brush
- Fine-grade sandpaper
- Deep red acrylic paint
- Matt water-based varnish
- Clear wax
- Soft cloth

This chest will probably be familiar to many of you as it comes from a well-known furnishing store and is very inexpensive. Judging by the number of times I have come across this chest, both decorated and in the raw, I would guess they have sold many thousands, so thinking of an original way to decorate it presented a challenge. The drawer arrangement on the chest is unusual and attempting individual decoration of each drawer could look uneven. I felt that the answer lay in treating the piece as a whole so I worked out a design that, with the help of a photocopier, fitted neatly between the top and bottom of each drawer. The design was adapted from a traditional Indian embroidery design and the red and white colouring I have used gives it an appealing freshness. The design was transferred to the chest using a transfer paper which comes in various colours. I have used a red paper, close in colour to the paint and completely invisible once the chest has been lightly sanded.

This project is more time consuming than many of the others in this book, but not at all difficult. You do not need to be an artist to fill in a transferred design with one solid colour, but a steady hand helps, so have a glass of wine when you have finished painting rather than before you start!

1 Paint the entire chest with two coats of red emulsion paint, allowing the first coat to dry before applying the second. Then, when this is dry, paint two coats of white emulsion paint over the top of the chest.

2 Rub the white paint lightly with sandpaper so that a hint of red shows through, particularly around the edges of the chest where it would naturally wear. Link the two middle drawers together with masking tape, avoiding the surface to be decorated. Repeat for the three top drawers. This stops any movement between the drawers and enables them to be treated as one surface.

3 Trace the design from the template (see p.88) and place the tracing paper in position on the chest. Slide a piece of transfer paper underneath and secure the design in place with masking tape. Transfer the design by drawing over it with a pencil. Do not remove the tracing paper until you have transferred all of the design, as it is very difficult to reposition it accurately. Continue in the same way for the remaining areas of the chest.

4 Using a fine-pointed artist's brush, carefully fill in the design with deep red acrylic paint. When the paint has dried, rub it lightly with wire wool to distress it.

5 Finish the chest by brushing it with a coat of matt water-based varnish and applying a clear wax over this. Buff to a shine with a soft cloth.

Découpaged bathroom cabinet

You will need:
- Coarse-grade sandpaper
- General-purpose acrylic *or* oil-based primer
- Paint brushes
- Emulsion *or* traditional paint in 2 colours
- Masking tape (optional)
- Paper images of fish and shells
- Manicure scissors
- Glue brush
- Paper glue
- Sponge
- Satin water-based varnish
- Varnish brush
- White emulsion paint
- Raw umber powder pigment
- Water
- Kitchen paper
- Medium-grade finishing paper

Is there anyone, I wonder, who does not have at least one piece of furniture made from whiteboard? I can own up to a few, bought with a mind firmly fixed on economy and practicality. Whiteboard furniture can be painted if you prepare it well and apply two or three coats of varnish over the paint to protect it.

To découpage is to cut out a printed image. The image is then glued on to a surface and given several coats of varnish, so that the impression is given that the surface has been handpainted. The technique was particularly popular in the 17th and 18th centuries as a pastime for the ladies of the French and Italian courts. Its popularity continued into Victorian times, which saw the advent of colour printing and the production of dye-cut scraps. These were used to decorate all manner of things and are still available today. By the beginning of the first world war, découpage had all but died out. However, it is presently enjoying a huge revival and the wonderful choice of giftwraps and printed images we now have make it a wonderfully creative process. The many layers of varnish that form part of the découpage process provide a good durable finish and make it an

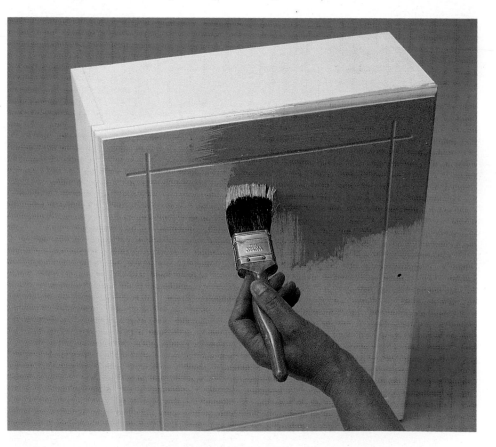

1 Roughen the surface of the cupboard with a coarse-grade sandpaper so that the paint will adhere more readily, then brush on the general-purpose primer and leave to dry. Paint over the primer with your choice of paint colour for the base coat.

ideal choice of treatment for a bathroom cabinet. I have used a combination of fishy wrapping paper I brought back from a holiday abroad and some 18th-century shell prints cut out from a book. There are several books available containing black and white prints of fish and shells (see p.94) which can be tinted using coloured pencils or watercolours.

I tested a number of acrylic primers for this project and some were more effective than others. Scratch the dried primer to test whether it is any good. If you can easily scratch the primer off the whiteboard surface with a fingernail, it is not suitable. A general-purpose oil-based primer is a good alternative. When you wipe off the antiquing paint that is used on the cupboard, some of it remains in the brushmarks left by the primer. By painting in the direction that you would normally expect the grain to go on a wooden cabinet, you can create the illusion that it is made from wood. I painted the cupboard in shades of blue and changed the knob to an ammonite one to complete the sealife theme.

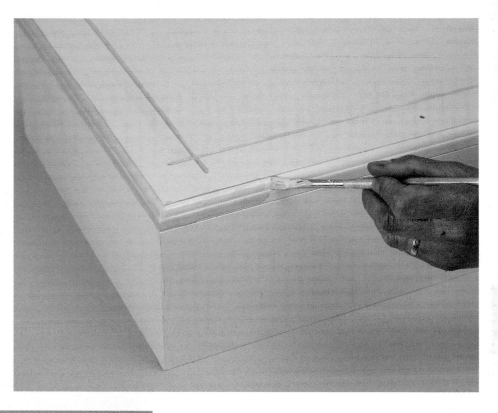

2 When dry, pick out the indented line with a contrasting colour of paint and a fine paint brush. If your cabinet does not have an indented line, mark out a border between two rows of masking tape and paint in between the rows.

3 Cut out a number of fish and shell images using a sharp pair of manicure scissors. Start experimenting with the design, arranging and re-arranging the images on the cabinet, and choosing the prints you want to finally use.

4 Brush the glue on to the cupboard, place a paper cut-out over this and press firmly into position. Look at the cupboard under a good light to make sure there are no bubbles of trapped air under the cut-outs which will spoil the finished appearance. Continue to stick all the remaining fish and shells down, then wash off the excess glue with a damp sponge and leave to dry for at least two hours. Check that all the edges are well stuck down, then varnish all the painted areas of the cupboard with two coats of satin varnish, leaving two hours between each coat. It is important that these first two coats are applied thinly, otherwise the paper might lift and bubble.

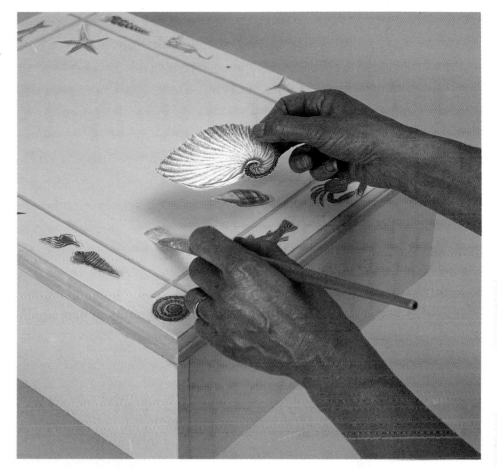

5 Mix together 1 teaspoon of white emulsion paint and 3 teaspoons of raw umber pigment and dilute this with water to make a thin, dark brown paint. Brush it over one side of the cupboard and leave it for a minute or two before wiping it off with a piece of kitchen paper. Repeat the process on each of the other sides. Varnish all the painted surfaces of the cupboard to seal the antiquing paint, then continue to varnish the découpaged door only with eight to ten more coats, depending on the thickness of the paper you have used and the finish you require. Sand the varnished surface with a medium-grade finishing paper, then apply a final coat of varnish.

Handprinted blanket box

You will need:
- Rubber gloves
- Soft cloths
- Dark brown french enamel varnish *or* water-based woodstain and clear shellac
- Kitchen paper
- Liquid wax
- Brush for applying wax
- Emulsion *or* traditional paint in 2 colours
- Paint brushes
- Water-soluble pencil
- Cardboard
- Ruler
- Scalpel knife
- Flexible masking tape
- 00 grade wire wool
- Medium-grade sandpaper
- Baby's bath sponge
- Plate
- Gold paint
- Alphabet tracing (see p.90)
- Transfer paper
- Brown wax

I used to wonder what the point was of printing a simple shape when you could just as easily stencil it. Well, the answer is that you can be much more spontaneous, freer with positioning and it is incredibly quick. The end result really has quite a different quality. However, if you prefer to have an even design, you can make a stencil of three or four oak leaves and cut them out to form a border. You will then need to mark horizontal and vertical lines on to the blanket box with a pencil, where you want to position the border. Begin stencilling by placing the centre of the stencil in the middle of a pencilled line and work out towards each end.

Painted betrothal chests were traditional in Europe for centuries and they would often include the bride's initials and date of marriage. Although the design I have used is not traditional, the use of a painted panel, the oak leaf motif and the printing technique are. Today, the blanket box would make an original personalized wedding gift, which not only looks attractive, but could also prove very useful for storing the towels, tablecloths and other linen one so often receives in excess at the start of a marriage. This project could even be adapted to make a lovely birth or christening present, by varying the colouring and decorating the chest with the child's initials and date of birth. It could first be used to store baby clothes and linen then, later on, to store toys.

I have used a similar ageing process on this chest to the one I used on the Antiqued kitchen cupboard (see

1 Wearing rubber gloves and using a soft cloth, stain the chest by rubbing french enamel varnish over the surface; alternatively, you can apply woodstain using kitchen paper. If you use a woodstain, go over it with clear shellac.

p.30), the difference being that I have started off with something completely new. Distressing the paint to reveal new natural pine would not look very convincing, so I have stained the chest with a dark brown french enamel varnish. This is shellac based and therefore seals the wood at the same time. A water-based woodstain and a coat of clear shellac make an equally successful alternative. You could draw the panel straight on to the chest without using a template if you prefer. However, the advantage of the template is that it can be used more than once and you can paint it and try out your design before transferring it to the chest. I drew around some paint tins to get the curves for the template and made the oak leaf print by drawing the shape on to a baby's bath sponge and cutting it out with a scalpel knife. Close-textured sponges that are sold damp and sealed with polythene are the best for this. I made the gold paint myself using a deep gold bronzing powder and an artist's acrylic medium to get the shade and degree of lustre that I wanted, but you can use any variety of commercially available gold paint.

2 Apply liquid wax with a brush over areas that would naturally wear, in addition to some other places. Then, when dry, paint the chest in your main choice of colour.

3 Draw your panel shape on to a piece of cardboard and use a ruler to make sure all your measurements are accurate. Cut the template out using a scalpel knife. Position the template in the centre of the chest, checking that it is accurately placed and draw around it with a pencil.

4 Mask the panel, using flexible masking tape where necessary, and paint inside it with the second colour of paint. Remove the tape and rub back the whole of the chest with wire wool and sandpaper.

5 Cut an oak leaf shape from the sponge. Brush some of the darker coloured paint on to a plate, dip the sponge into this and press it down flat on the edge of the chest. Continue in this way until you have formed a border. Print in gold over the existing oak leaves using the same process.

6 Transfer the initials and dates on to the central panel using transfer paper as described in the Handpainted chest (see p. 40). Using a fine brush, paint a gold line over the darker colour around the edge of the panel. Then fill in the lettering.

7 Apply a coat of brown wax to the chest with a cloth; leave it for about half an hour before buffing it. If you have used chalky paints, as I have done, this will totally transform the appearance of the chest and bring out the richness of colour.

Chequered table and chair

You will need:
- Cloth
- Detergent
- Water
- Medium- and fine-grade sandpaper
- Wood filler
- Filling knife
- White emulsion paint
- Paint brushes
- Masking tape
- Water-soluble pencil
- Ruler
- Emulsion *or* traditional paint in 3 colours
- Satin *or* matt water-based varnish
- Varnish brush

The table and chairs used for this project had been discarded by a nursery school and cost me less than £5 for the lot. I bought them for my children when they were younger, intending to decorate them, but somehow was always too busy to do so. Finally completed, they are now promised to the first of my children to produce a grandchild! I liked the idea of painting a colourful design that would appeal to small children and one that they wouldn't outgrow as they got older. It is nice to use different colours for the chairs and these colours are then incorporated into the table design by painting the odd diamond shape in one of them. The design was quite complicated to work out so that it fitted the pieces exactly but, if you don't quite feel up to it, a chequered pattern in line with the table or placed diagonally would be easier to mark out than the harlequin one and would make a good alternative. If you are feeling ambitious, you could continue the harlequin theme by painting the walls of the nursery with different-sized diamonds, placed at random.

1 Using a cloth, detergent and water, wash the table and chairs, making sure they are thoroughly clean and free of grease. Rub all the surfaces well with a medium-grade sandpaper and fill all the holes with wood filler. Paint the table and chairs with three coats of white emulsion paint to ensure good coverage. Allow each coat to dry thoroughly before applying the next. Make sure the final coat is smooth by sanding it with a fine-grade sandpaper, then stick masking tape around the edges of the table, the seat and the back of each chair.

2 *Mark out the design on the table. Do this by deciding on the approximate size of the diamonds you require and work out how many will fit along the top and down the sides of the table. I planned six complete diamond shapes both across and down the table. Mark the width of the table with a series of dots where the point of the diamond will go and the length of the table in the same way. Join up the first dot along the width with the first dot along the length using a water-soluble pencil and ruler, and continue in this way until you have covered the full length of the table. Repeat this process starting from the opposite side and so forming a diamond pattern. Mark the design on the chairs. This time you only need to decide how many diamonds you want across the width of the chair back, making sure the design is centred.*

3 *Separate alternate diamond shapes on the tabletop using strips of masking tape.*

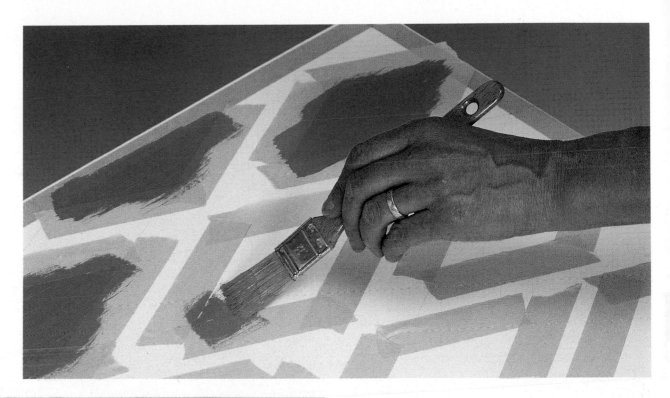

4 Paint the diamonds in the colour of your choice, brushing in the direction of the grain of the wood. When these are dry, mask the remaining diamonds and fill in with more colour, this time incorporating the colours in the chairs in a random way. If you are uncertain where to place the colour, paint some lining paper with the different-coloured paints, cut out diamond shapes the same size as on the table and try out different arrangements until you find one that you are happy with.

5 Place a second row of masking tape just inside the first, then remove the tape next to the edge of the table. Paint this in the main colour of the table. Fill in the diamond shapes on the chairs and paint the border around the edges. Wipe off all the pencil marks with a damp cloth. Using a medium-grade sandpaper, rub over the painted surface to soften the effect. Finally, protect the furniture with two coats of satin or matt water-based varnish, allowing the first coat to dry before applying the second.

Scumble-glazed table

Scandinavian painted furniture has become enormously popular recently and is noted for its elegant simple styling. The soft blue-grey I have used on this table is typical of colouring used on Swedish neo-classical furniture. The subtle dragged effect was achieved using a flat varnish brush and a transparent water-based scumble glaze mixed with acrylic paint. This replaces the oil-based glazes used traditionally and has the added advantage of being quicker drying and non-yellowing. The scumble takes two to four hours to dry so you need to avoid painting a surface adjoining one you have just worked on for that length of time or you will spoil the finish. The glaze needs a non-absorbent surface and I have used a very pale grey satin emulsion paint for the table, which has an MDF top and pine legs. I used equal quantities of ivory black, prussion blue and titanium white for the glaze mix and the same colours without the glaze for painting around the edge. The gilt cream I have used for the edge works more effectively over a deep-coloured base.

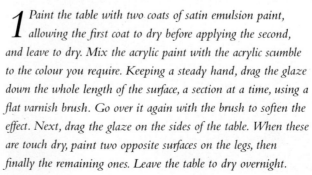

1 Paint the table with two coats of satin emulsion paint, allowing the first coat to dry before applying the second, and leave to dry. Mix the acrylic paint with the acrylic scumble to the colour you require. Keeping a steady hand, drag the glaze down the whole length of the surface, a section at a time, using a flat varnish brush. Go over it again with the brush to soften the effect. Next, drag the glaze on the sides of the table. When these are touch dry, paint two opposite surfaces on the legs, then finally the remaining ones. Leave the table to dry overnight.

2 Make an antiquing wash by mixing 1 teaspoon PVA medium or glue with 2 teaspoons rottenstone and 250ml (8fl oz) water. Alternatively, dilute some raw umber acrylic paint with water. Brush this on the surface of the table a section at a time, then wipe it off with kitchen paper, so as to leave a soft aged effect. If you attempt the whole table surface at once the finish is likely to be patchy unless you work extremely quickly. Complete the rest of the table in the same way.

3 Paint the border on the tabletop and around the drawer with your choice of acrylic colour without any added glaze. I have used a mixture of ivory black, prussian blue, and titanium white satin emulsion.

4 Brush the gilt cream over the borders, leave it to dry and buff with a soft cloth. Varnish the table apart from the gold edges with two coats of matt water-based varnish to protect it, allowing the first coat to dry before applying the second.

Craquelure lamp base

You will need:

- White emulsion paint
- Paint brushes
- Flexible masking tape
- Acrylic scumble
- Water
- Acrylic paint
- Stencil brush
- Water-based varnish
- Varnish brush
- Two-part crackle varnish
- Soft synthetic brush
- Raw umber artist's oil colour
- White spirit
- Kitchen paper
- Satin oil-based varnish

Painted lamp bases, like this one, always seem to me to be extraordinarily expensive. Once you have mastered the craquelure technique, you will find it quick and simple to do and you can delight in the large amount of money saved. This cracked porcelain effect is achieved by brushing on two different varnishes, a slow-drying oil varnish followed by a quick-drying water-soluble one, then rubbing in oil colour so that the cracks are clearly visible. The effect is enormously popular and can be very successfully used to create an aged appearance over paint as well as over handpainted, découpaged and stencilled designs. Unfortunately, the manufacturers of

these two-part varnishes do not provide very comprehensive instructions with their product and I have found that a large number of my students have had great difficulty in making the technique work. I have probably received more requests to demonstrate this effect than any other and I hope that the following information and step-by-step instructions will help to demystify the process. The results are never quite predictable, but if you take note of the following, they will be more so.

Provide a good base for the craquelure by sealing your decorated item with a coat of water-based varnish. Avoid using this technique on a rainy or humid day as

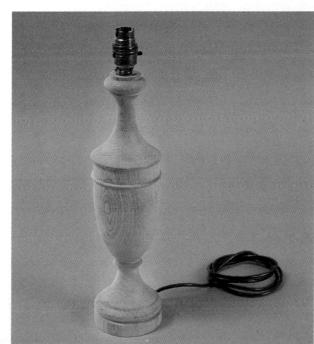

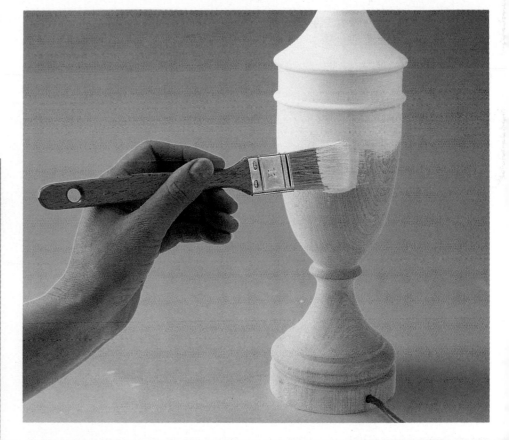

1 Using a household brush, paint the lamp base with two or three coats of white emulsion paint, allowing each coat to dry thoroughly before applying the next.

the cracks will need a considerable amount of encouragement to appear! A hair dryer can assist the process but use it on a gentle setting or you will finish up with an unnatural looking crazing as you also will if you leave your work in a hot sunny window. Leaving your decorated piece near a radiator or in an airing cupboard is usually effective.

The size of the cracks depends on how thickly you apply both layers of varnish. The thinner the layers, the smaller the cracks will be. The length of time between applying the two coats also affects the size, with a longer amount of time resulting in finer cracks. You could practise this technique first on cardboard which has been sealed with water-based varnish; if you get into trouble you can remove the raw umber paint with white spirit, wash off the water varnish and leave it to dry before starting again. You need to remember that the second varnish is water soluble and care must be taken not to get it wet or touch it with damp or clammy

2 Stick masking tape above and below the bands around the lamp where you want a contrasting colour, using flexible masking tape over the curved surfaces. Mix a little acrylic scumble and water with some acrylic paint and stipple on the colour with a stencil brush. Leave to dry for about four hours, then seal the whole lamp with a coat of water-based varnish and let it dry thoroughly.

3 Brush the oil-based cracking varnish evenly over the lamp, holding it to the light to make sure you have covered it all. Leave this to dry, usually for between two and four hours, until it feels dry when you glide the back of your finger over the surface, but is still just tacky when you press your knuckle to it. Brush on the water-soluble cracking varnish with a soft-haired synthetic brush so as not to leave any brush marks. Make sure that you have covered every part of the first coat by holding it to a light. Leave this for about half an hour to dry, then check to see if there are any areas you have missed and cover them with more of the second coat if you have. Any missed areas that go unspotted result in dark patches.

hands. This second varnish is finally sealed with an oil-based varnish once the oil colour that is used to reveal the cracks has dried.

I have painted the lamp base here with a plain white emulsion paint, an effective background colour as it makes the cracks highly visible and will finish up looking cream. The bands of colour are a mixture of venetian red and burnt umber acrylic paints mixed with acrylic scumble; they have been stippled on with a stencil brush.

Finally, a parchment lampshade, a type that is widely available from many good department stores, was chosen for this lamp base. It was first sealed with a layer of water-based varnish, then it was given the same craquelure treatment as the lamp base. However, in order to retain the matt appearance that the parchment originally had, I sealed the lampshade with a final coat of dead flat varnish, instead of the satin varnish which I used for the base.

4 *The cracks should appear as soon as the second varnish has dried, although they are hard to see at this stage. If they do not appear, leave the lamp base in a warm place or apply a gentle heat until they appear. Dilute some raw umber artist's oil colour with a little white spirit so that it has a creamy texture and rub this into the surface with kitchen paper. Take a clean piece of kitchen paper and wipe it off, leaving the raw umber paint remaining in the cracks.*

5 *Add a little more white spirit to the raw umber and dip a stencil brush into it. Run your index finger through the bristles to spray the surface of the lamp base with fine spatters. Soften the effect by dabbing it with a piece of kitchen paper. Leave the lamp to dry overnight, then seal it with a coat of satin oil-based varnish.*

*S*tencilled bedside chest

You will need:

- White acrylic wood primer
- Paint brushes
- Pink and green traditional *or* emulsion paint
- 00 grade wire wool
- Photocopies of stencils (see p.88)
- Stencil film and pencil *or* acetate and pen
- Cutting mat *or* thick cardboard
- Scalpel knife
- Masking tape
- Acrylic paint in 2 shades each of pink and green
- Paint palette *or* plate
- Stencil brush
- Kitchen paper
- Liming wax
- Soft cloth

Stencilling is enormously popular and I expect many of you will already have tried your hand at it. It is a wonderfully quick and versatile way of creating pattern and form, and there is a huge range of ready-made stencils now on the market, obtainable from DIY stores as well as from specialist shops. Additionally, there are a number of books containing a wide range of copyright-free designs which can be traced on to stencil film. An address for these can be found in the list of suppliers (see p.94). Of course, you may like to design your own stencil. Starting from scratch does require a degree of drawing skill, but it is relatively simple to adapt an existing image into a stencil design by simplifying where

necessary and creating 'bridges'. If you want to decorate your bedside chest by incorporating a design that appears on your bedroom curtains, for example, you can photocopy a section of the fabric, enlarging or reducing it as required. You can then trace appropriate elements and turn these into a stencil design.

This new pine chest has been stencilled using the two stencils shown on p.88. I have used different elements of the design to create my own arrangements and make each drawer and the chest top individual. The drawers do not need to be placed in any particular order; you can arrange them how you please. The way I approached this was to take several photocopies of the

1 Prime the bedside chest with a coat of white acrylic primer. Leave to dry thoroughly, then paint the whole chest, including all three drawers, with one coat of pink traditional paint and leave to dry overnight.

two stencils, cut them up into different sections, and arrange them on the chest until I found a design that was pleasing. I then placed the cut stencil over the photocopy, removed the design and marked the position lightly with a pencil.

You can use many different types of paint for stencilling and not just those sold for the purpose. I have chosen acrylic paints for this project because they are strongly coloured and will not disappear under the liming wax, but instead become very subtle. For me, the number one rule when stencilling is 'less is best' – less paint that is. Keep plenty of kitchen paper handy for dabbing off the excess paint on your stencil brushes. Using two shades of pink for the roses and two greens for the stems and leaves gives a shaded effect to the colour and adds more depth. I used traditional chalky paints for the background colour on the chest. These colours would normally darken when varnished or waxed, but by applying liming wax to the paint the pale chalky quality is retained.

2 Paint one coat of green traditional paint over the pink paint around the edges of the drawers, holding the paint brush steady so that you don't get paint on the front of the drawers. Then paint the chest top and the rest of the chest.

3 Rub wire wool over the painted surface so that a hint of white primer shows through the pink paint and a hint of pink shows through the green. Trace the rose stencil designs on to stencil film with a pencil or with a suitable pen if you choose acetate. Place the tracing on a cutting mat or a piece of thick cardboard to protect your work surface. Carefully cut out the design using a scalpel knife.

4 *Plan your design as described above. Place a stencil in position on the chest and secure it down with masking tape. If you like, you can mask out the areas on the stencil that you are not using. Put some of the paler pink acrylic paint on to the palette and dip the stencil brush in it. Wipe off all the excess paint on to a piece of kitchen paper so that the brush is almost dry, then paint through the stencil to fill in the roses with a stippling motion. Next fill in with the lighter green and then, more sparingly, the darker colours. Continue until you have completed all of your design.*

5 *Apply liming wax to the whole of the chest with a pad of kitchen paper and leave it to dry for half an hour. The wax will subdue the colour of the paint. Then polish the chest to a shine with a soft cloth.*

Gilded mirror frame

You will need:
- Wood glue *or* PVA glue
- Mouldings
- Wood filler
- Filling knife
- Masking tape
- Red ochre emulsion *or* traditional paint
- Various paint brushes
- Acrylic goldsize
- Transfer metal leaf
- Scissors
- Bronzing powder
- Brown shellac
- Rottenstone
- White emulsion *or* traditional paint
- 0000 grade wire wool
- Methylated spirit
- Water
- Clear *or* medium-brown wax
- Soft cloth

This is a new, very inexpensive, pine mirror that has taken on quite a different appearance by adding a few carved mouldings. I used wooden mouldings which were carved by apprentices and were among a selection I bought cheaply at a fair. I purchased them some time before the mirror and, by amazing good fortune, they fitted perfectly. Wood, plastic and plaster mouldings can all be found easily and used to give plain furniture a more decorative appearance.

The art of gilding, which is the application of very finely beaten sheets of metal to a surface, is thousands of years old. It must be said that fine quality gilding, using loose leaf, is a skill that needs a good deal of practice but many wonderful effects can be achieved by a beginner using transfer metal leaf.

Metal leaf comes in small squares, either loose which are difficult to handle, or backed with a sheet of waxed paper for transferring them to a surface. You can buy real gold and silver leaf, both of which are very expensive, but aluminium, copper, and bronze are also available, much less expensive and are obtainable from good art shops and specialist decorating suppliers.

1 Decide where you want to position the mouldings on your frame; I concentrated on the upper part of the frame. Then, using wood glue or PVA glue, stick the mouldings in place. Fill any gaps in the frame with wood filler.

Traditionally, either oil size or a watery glue size is applied over several layers of gesso on the surface to receive the leaf. Gilding with transfer leaf over oil size is easy once the oil size has dried to the right tack. If the size is too wet, the leaf loses its lustre; if it is too dry, then the leaf will not stick.

However, there is no need to panic, and you can relax, as gilding has become simpler in recent times with the introduction of acrylic goldsize. While this is not suitable for the highest quality work, it is more than adequate for most decorative purposes. Acrylic size has the advantage of being ready to gild over in about 15 minutes and stays tacky indefinitely. It is very easy to apply and is also inexpensive.

Bronzing powders can also be applied over tacky size. They come in a wide range of colours and, while they do not have the lustre of metal leaf, they are extremely useful for filling in cracks in the leaf which are inevitable when gilding a carved surface. Both metal leaf and bronzing powders need to be sealed with a coat of shellac or varnish to prevent tarnishing. I have used a red ochre paint to imitate red bole or clay which is traditionally used as a base for gold leaf.

2 Stick masking tape all around the mirror edge to keep it clean, then paint the whole of the frame with two coats of red ochre paint, allowing the first coat to dry thoroughly before applying the next. Leave to dry.

3 Using a soft synthetic brush, apply acrylic goldsize to the mouldings on the frame. It will appear milky at this stage but it soon becomes transparent. After 15 to 20 minutes, when the goldsize is completely clear, it is ready to gild over.

4 Cut a sheet of transfer metal leaf in half with a pair of scissors and place this over the goldsize. Tamp the leaf down with a firm-bristled brush so that it goes into the recessed areas as well as on the surface. Lift the backing paper off and continue in this way, using all remaining scraps on the sheets to fill in small gaps. When you have covered the mouldings as much as you can, dust them with bronzing powder to fill any remaining gaps.

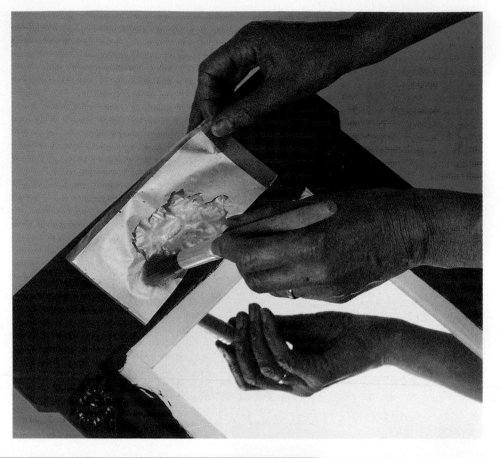

5 Gently brush a coat of brown shellac over the gilded mouldings to seal and age the metal leaf. You can add a little rottenstone to the shellac, as I have done, to give the frame a slightly more aged effect.

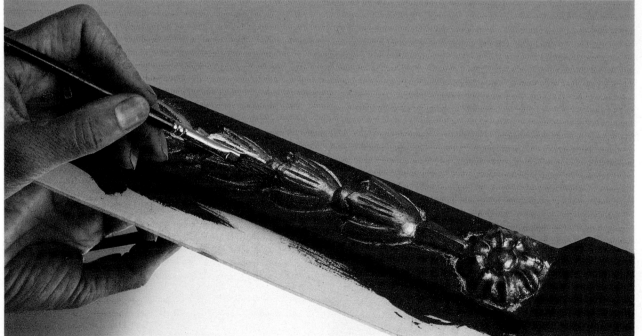

6 Paint the remainder of the frame with two coats of white paint over the red, allowing the first coat to dry before applying the second. When this is dry, rub down the painted surface here and there with 0000 grade wire wool dipped in methylated spirit. If you have used a soft traditional paint, as I have done, wire wool and water are sufficient.

7 Mix some rottenstone with liquid clear wax and apply it to the frame, using a small brush to reach right up to the mouldings. If you prefer, you can substitute this with a medium-brown wax. Leave the wax to dry, then polish the frame with a soft cloth.

Verdigris metal table

You will need:
- Methylated spirit
- Kitchen paper *or* rag
- Rust-inhibiting metal primer
- Paint brushes
- Water-based gold paint
- Brown shellac *or* french enamel varnish
- Varnish brush
- Blue-green emulsion paint
- Stencil brush
- Mint-green emulsion paint
- Mutton cloth
- Off-white emulsion paint
- Acrylic paint in 2 shades
- Acrylic scumble
- Water
- Water-soluble pencil
- Ruler
- Straight edge *or* long ruler
- Masking tape
- Satin water-based varnish

Round metal tables are inexpensive, easily found and can be really transformed with a painted finish. The one I have used here is unpainted, but if yours is painted sand it with a coarse sandpaper to roughen its surface, then follow the instructions as below. A verdigris effect is an appropriate choice for a piece of metal furniture and here I have restricted it to the base, choosing a star design for the top over glazes of yellow ochre and raw sienna. By using deeper tones of colours similar to those already used, the choice of colour for the star gives unity to the table design as a whole. Alternate sections of the star were painted with the ochre mixed with raw umber and Hooker's green mixed with cobalt blue. Although this table was photographed outside, it would not be suitable for leaving outdoors.

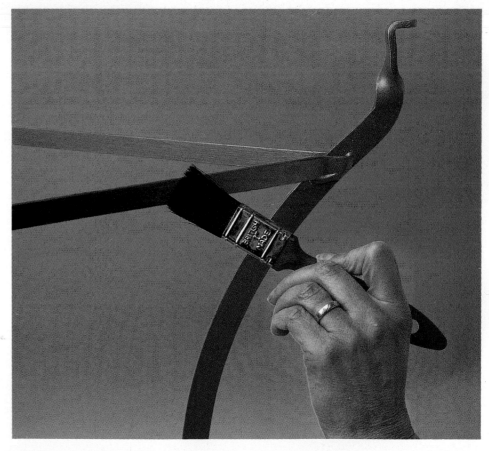

1 Degrease the table by wiping it with methylated spirit using kitchen paper or a rag. Prime the table with the rust-inhibiting metal primer and, when it is dry, paint over it with gold paint.

2 Leave the gold paint to dry. Then paint brown shellac or french enamel varnish over the top to tone it down.

3 When the shellac or varnish is dry, apply blue-green paint sparingly with a stencil brush, using a stippling motion for a textured effect. Leave to dry.

4 Using the stencil brush, dab mint-green paint slightly more generously over the top of the blue-green paint, allowing patches of blue-green paint to show through.

5 Dip a piece of mutton cloth in methylated spirit and dab this over the stippled paint to blend it. If you prefer, you can dab on a dilute wash of dark green acrylic paint and water to strengthen the colour a little.

6 Paint the tabletop with two or three coats of off-white emulsion paint, allowing each coat to dry thoroughly before applying the next. This provides a more subtle base than brilliant white.

7 Mix two slightly different shades of acrylic paint with acrylic scumble. Add a little water to each so that they become both less jelly-like and able to hold the brush marks. Brush a thin layer of one colour lightly and in a random way over the tabletop, so as not to leave obvious brush marks in any particular direction. If you want to eliminate the brushstrokes altogether, dab the surface with a mutton cloth. Leave this to dry then brush on the second colour. This process can be repeated until you have the shade you require. Using two colours gives added depth and interest.

8 Mark out the design for the star as shown in the diagram on p.91 using a water-soluble pencil, ruler and straight edge or long ruler. Draw a line through the centre and a second at right angles. Divide into eight equal segments. Take an equal measurement on each line from the centre to about 1.5cm (⅝in) from the edge and mark with a dot. Join up the dots with lines as shown. When all the lines are completed, wipe out those which do not form part of the final design.

9 Paint the segments of the star with your choice of acrylic colours mixed with acrylic scumble, using masking tape around the area to be painted. Dab the surface with a piece of mutton cloth to give a subtle transparent appearance. Protect the table surface with a satin or matt water-based varnish.

Lined clock cupboard

You will need:

- Medium-grade sandpaper
- Wood filler
- Filling knife
- Emulsion *or* traditional paint in 3 shades
- Paint brushes
- Masking tape (optional)
- Pencil
- Ruler
- Sword liner *or* fine brush
- Fruit print
- Manicure scissors
- Paper glue
- Glue brush
- Sponge
- Satin water-based acrylic varnish
- Varnish brush
- Two-part craquelure varnish
- Kitchen paper
- Raw umber pigment
- Matt oil-based varnish
- Brown wax
- Soft cloth

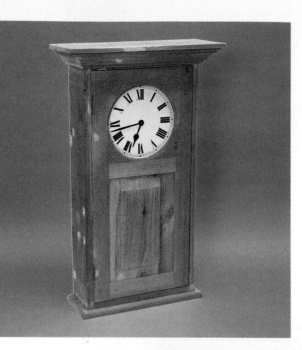

This attractive wall cupboard is new but has been made from old pine floorboards. The clock face is simply cardboard which is transformed by using a craquelure technique. This piece of furniture has strong simple lines which I felt would be spoilt by over-fussy decoration. I decided upon a découpaged pear motif for the door panel, which is appropriate for kitchen use and the three tones of yellow were chosen with this lovely 18th-century print in mind. I started with the middle tone of creamy yellow and added white to this to paint the central panel. The paint for the darker panel surround was made with the addition of raw umber pigment. A lining technique has been used on the cupboard; I like to use a sword liner for this because it holds a good amount of paint for a continuous flow. It is also economical because you only need one brush to produce a variety of line sizes, as the width of a line is determined

1 Rub the cupboard well with a medium-grade sandpaper to smooth it down, then fill all the holes and cracks with a wood filler. Paint all the cupboard, except for the door panel, with a coat of the middle tone of paint, and then paint the central panel with the light tone. When dry, paint the panel surround with the darkest colour. It is not usually necessary to use masking tape when painting a raised or recessed surface, but you can do so if you find it easier.

2 *Using a pencil and ruler, lightly mark the clock where you want to position the narrow lines. Load a sword liner brush with the dark paint colour and drag the brush along the pencilled line.*

3 *Cut out the print with a pair of manicure scissors. Glue it on to the panel and press it into place. Wash off the excess glue with a damp sponge. Leave the print to dry, then disguise any white edges on the cut-out by going over them with a pencil.*

by the pressure used when applying the paint to a surface. These brushes are available from specialist decorating suppliers, but if you have difficulty in obtaining one, use a 6mm (¼in) long-haired flat artist's brush instead. It is a good idea to paint a sample board on which to practise your lines before you apply them to furniture. Because the wood is old, it is not necessary to prime it but you may find the grain becomes raised in areas after the first coat of paint and will require sanding before the second one is applied.

4 *Brush two coats of acrylic varnish over the entire cupboard, then a further eight to ten coats over the découpaged panel only, allowing each coat to dry thoroughly before applying the next. Seal the clock face with a coat of acrylic varnish, then apply the two cracking varnishes as described in the Craquelure lamp base (see p.58). Using kitchen paper, rub in the raw umber pigment when the second coat is dry, then seal the surface with a matt oil-based varnish the next day. Using kitchen paper, apply a brown wax over the entire surface of the cupboard, including the clock face. Leave this to dry for about half an hour, then polish with a soft cloth.*

Lacquered butler's tray

You will need:
- Coarse-grade sandpaper
- Sanding block
- Acrylic wood primer
- Paint brushes
- Black traditional paint
- Water-based varnish
- Varnish brush
- Lacquer-red traditional paint
- 0000 grade wire wool
- Methylated spirit *or* water
- Shellac *or* spray varnish
- Brush for applying shellac
- Ruler
- Pencil
- Masking tape
- Tracing paper
- Talcum powder
- Acrylic goldsize
- Bronzing powder
- Cotton wool
- Clear wax
- Oil-based varnish (optional)

The paint technique I have used for this tray is meant to give the impression of oriental lacquerwork, particularly by the choice of colour. I have not set out to create an authentic look as this would be impossible to do with paint. Real lacquerwork has been practised for centuries by very skilled craftsmen, who apply dozens of layers of coloured lacquer made from the sap of a type of gum tree. The surface is then decorated or carved to reveal the lower layers. Nowadays this technique is usually done with many layers of shellac and pigment over a gesso base. It is still a very lengthy process.

A book of ancient Chinese ornament was the inspiration behind the design on the tray, the larger central motif having been adapted from the decoration on a plate. I simplified a Chinese key design to create the

1 Roughen the highly varnished surface of the tray by sanding it with a coarse-grade sandpaper wrapped around a sanding block. Rub the tray in a circular motion, applying even pressure to remove as much of the shine as possible. Wipe down the sanded surface to remove dust.

border. The design as a whole continues the oriental theme without overstating it and therefore will fit comfortably into present day decorating schemes.

The lacquer technique I have used, though many layered, is quick and simple. A varnish layer is applied over the black paint to make certain that when the red paint is distressed, none of the white primer becomes visible. The bronze powder work is rather more painstaking and is best tackled a small area at a time. The process involves accurately painting acrylic goldsize over a transferred design and then carefully applying the powder with a fine brush. If you paint the size over too large an area of the design at once, it is likely to get marked. In particular, you need to take care that you do not smudge the talcum powder over the size as the bronzing powder will not adhere if you do. If you prefer, you could paint on the design with gold paint or even stencil it. Both would look very effective but would not have the lustre or the subtlety of shading that the bronze powders have.

2 Paint the tray with a coat of acrylic wood primer. Leave to dry.

3 Paint the tray with two coats of black paint, allowing the first coat to dry thoroughly before applying the second. Then brush one coat of water-based varnish over this to seal it.

4 Leave the varnish to dry for several hours, then paint two coats of red paint over the tray top and legs, allowing the first coat to dry before applying the second. Leave to dry.

5 Rub down the surface of the red paint with fine wire wool dipped in methylated spirit. If you have used traditional chalky paints, as I have done, wire wool and water are sufficient Do not over-do this process, particularly on the tray surface. Try rubbing the wire wool in a circular motion to avoid picking up obvious brush mark lines. Seal the tray with clear shellac.

6 Measure each side of the tray and mark the centre of each side with a pencil dot. Place a ruler on the pairs of opposite dots to find the centre of the tray and mark this with a dot also. Place the circular design (see p. 92) in the centre of the tray and secure it with masking tape. Trace over the design with a hard pencil, pressing firmly, and remove the tracing paper. Work out how many segments of the key border will fit around the tray, measuring from the centre of each side towards each corner. The corner key adds a nice touch but doesn't have to be used. Transfer the border on to the tray with a pencil in the same way. Dust the tray with talcum powder and spread it over the tray with a soft brush. This makes the pencil marks visible and prevents the possibility of the gold powder sticking to any other area than the sized one.

7 Carefully paint the centre of the design with acrylic goldsize, using a fine paint brush, and leave for 15 to 20 minutes for the size to become tacky.

8 Using a fine soft brush, dust bronzing powder over the size. Do so more heavily in some areas than others. Continue in this way until you have completed all the decoration on the tray.

9 Stick two rows of masking tape on the top edging of the tray. Brush the acrylic goldsize between the lines of tape; when this has dried clear, dust with bronzing powder.

10 Remove all the excess gold and talcum powder from the tray with a damp cotton wool pad. You need to be very gentle when doing this or you will remove the design, but it is important to remove all traces of powder before proceeding to the next stage. Seal the decorated surfaces by brushing on a coat of shellac, taking care not to overbrush any area, or use spray varnish. Then protect the tray with two coats of matt water-based varnish. Finish with a clear wax polish and buff. If you want a more heat-resistant finish, use an oil-based varnish in place of the water-based one.

Frottaged and stencilled screen

You will need:
- Yellow emulsion *or* traditional paint
- Paint roller and tray
- Water-based gold paint
- Paint brushes
- Emulsion *or* traditional paint in colour of your choice
- Tissue paper
- Stencil film
- Scalpel knife
- Cutting mat *or* thick cardboard
- Flexible and straight masking tape
- Ruler
- Pencil
- Long ruler *or* straight edge
- Set square
- Stencil brush *or* natural sponge
- Kitchen paper
- Medium-grade finishing paper
- Matt water-based varnish

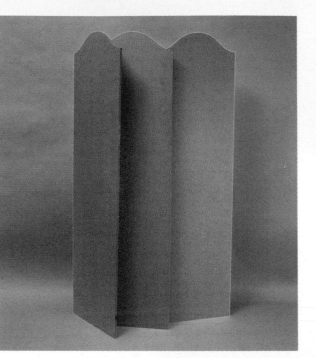

The idea of decorating a three-panelled screen can appear quite daunting, even to me! It is quite usual to decorate such screens with fabric and I have devised a way of using paint to give the impression that it has been covered in antique damask and surrounded by a ribbon border. It is, in a way, a *trompe-l'oeil* effect. Although there are numerous layers, each one is quick and simple. However, a word of warning: for the effect to be a success, it is absolutely essential that you mark out the vertical lines accurately and make sure that the horizontal ones line up on each of the panels.

The screen was made from MDF, which has a very smooth surface. To make the textile effect more realistic, texture had to be created by applying paint with a roller as a base to work on. Further texture was added later by pressing a sheet of tissue paper against the wet paint. This technique is known as frottage. I have copied many stencil designs from old damask to decorate walls, but

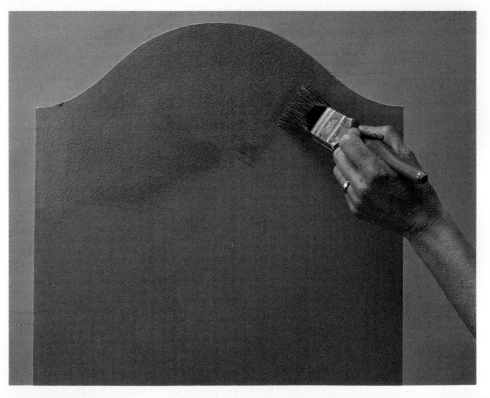

1 Create texture for the screen by applying two coats of yellow paint over the surface with a paint roller. Allow the first coat to dry thoroughly before applying the second. Yellow is a good colour to use because it helps to disguise any thin area in the final gold layer. Using a paint brush, apply two coats of gold paint over the yellow, allowing the first coat to dry thoroughly before applying the second.

the designs were all too large for this screen. In the end, I adapted my design from the embossed wallpaper below the dado rail in my hall. It is a simple repeat pattern that will fit different sizes of screen and, if you like, you could also use it on your walls. The colour I have chosen is a red ochre which looks so good with the gold, but deep shades of green or blue would also look very striking. Choose a good-quality gold paint with a high lustre, or make your own by mixing bronzing powder with an acrylic or PVA medium. The latter has the advantage of the choice from a wide range of gold colours. The stencilled area is quite big and you will find it much quicker to work with a large-sized stencil brush. Try to find one that is not too close-textured for greater flexibility and ease of use. Alternatively, you can use a natural sponge on a large stencil like this, but whether you are using a sponge or a brush, it is important to have plenty of kitchen paper handy for removing the excess paint.

2 When the gold paint has dried, paint the colour you have chosen over about one-third of one panel, using a large, wide paint brush.

3 Immediately press a sheet of tissue paper against the wet surface, pressing it flat with your hand, then peel it off. This creates a textured effect and loses all the brush marks. Complete the rest of this panel and the other two panels in the same way.

4 Trace the pattern on p.93 on to stencil film with a pencil and mark the line down the middle of the stencil. Cut out the design, including the registration marks (the little diamond on each corner) with a scalpel knife, using a cutting mat or thick cardboard to protect your work surface. Stick masking tape around each panel, using flexible tape for the curved area at the top. Draw a line down the centre of each panel exactly in the middle. To do this, make a series of dots at regular intervals down the length of each panel, checking that the distance between the dot and the edge of the panel on one side is equal to the distance on the other side. A centring ruler is very useful here. Join up all the dots with a light pencil line using a long ruler or straight edge. You will find it easier if you lay each panel on a flat surface for measuring and marking.

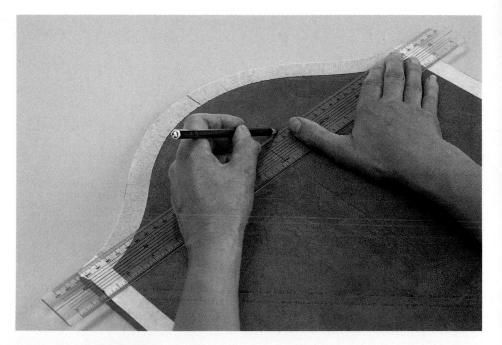

5 Draw a line across one of the panels near the top. Make sure that it is horizontal by checking its position in relation to the line down the centre, using a set square. Place another panel level next to it and continue the line in exactly the same position on this, then finally on the third panel.

6 Place the stencil in the position for starting, lining the centre of the stencil with the line down the middle of the screen. Secure with masking tape and draw a horizontal line on the stencil film to match that on the panel. This will ensure that the starting point is the same for each panel. Dip the stencil brush into the gold paint and wipe off the excess on a piece of kitchen paper. Dab the paint through the stencil, varying the amount you use to give a faded look. Make sure you dab a little paint through the diamond registration mark. You will need this to line up the next stencil. Don't worry that these registration marks will spoil your design; they will be lost in the overall effect. Move the stencil down the screen, lining up the diamonds at the top with gold ones stencilled at the bottom of the previous stencil. Continue down the panel and on the sides, matching up the registration marks. Stencil the pattern on all the panels in the same way.

7 Place a second row of masking tape just inside the existing
tape before removing it. Brush gold paint around the edge
of the screen. Use the paint sparingly with the brush fairly dry,
so that that red paint shows through.

8 Rub back the surface gently with a medium-grade
finishing paper, then seal the screen with a coat of matt
water-based varnish.

*T*emplates

Stencilled bedside chest, p.62 (Actual size)

Handpainted chest, p.40 (Actual size)

Stencilled bedside chest, p.62 (Actual size)

AABBCDDEEFFGG
HHIJJKKLLMM
NNOPPQQRRSSTT
ThUVUWWXYZZ

abcdee fghijkklm
nopqrstuvwxyz

1234567890

(&$$¢¢/.,.:;?!-""''*)

Oak leaf motif, p.47
(Actual size)

Enlarge alphabet by 250%

Handprinted blanket box, p.47

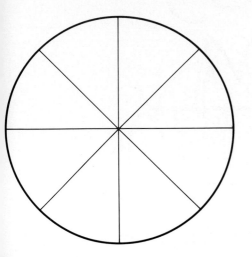 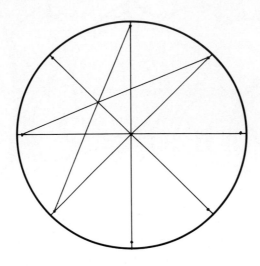 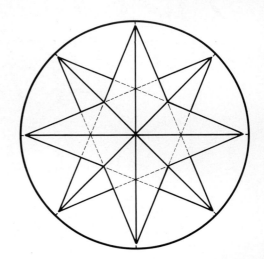

Star design for the Verdigris metal table, p.71

Lacquered butler's tray, p.78 (Actual size)

Laquered butler's tray, p.78 (Actual size)

Frottaged and stencilled screen, p.83

(Actual size)

Suppliers

Traditional paints
Pine Brush Products
Stockingate
Coton Clanford
Stafford ST18 9PB
Tel: 01785 282799
Colourman paints, shellac, water-based varnishes, waxes, crackle varnishes; and pine clock cupboards.

Relics (UK Distributors)
35 Bridge Street
Witney
Oxon OX8 6DA
Tel: 01993 704611
Annie Sloan's Traditional Paints.

Design books
Dover Bookshop
18 Earlham Street
London WC2H 9LP
Tel: 0171-836 2111
Books for découpage containing copyright-free designs from many historic sources.

Specialist decorating suppliers
Foxell and James
57 Farringdon Road
London EC1M 3JH
Tel: 0171-405 0152
Powdered pigments, rottenstone, crackle varnishes, acrylic scumble, shellac, waxes, water-based varnish, gilding supplies, brushes.

Papers and Paints
4 Park Walk
London SW10 0AD
Tel: 0171-352 8626
As previous address, including a range of historic paint colours.

Green and Stone
259 Kings Road
London SW3 5ER
Tel: 0171-352 0837

Plotons
273 Archway
London N6 5AA
Tel: 0181-348 0315

Brodie and Middleton
68 Drury Lane
London WC2 5SP
Tel: 0171-836 3289
French enamel varnish, powder pigments.

Furniture for painting
Scumble Goosie
Lewiston Mill
Toadsmore Road
Brimscombe, Stroud
Gloucestershire GL5 2TB
Tel: 01453 731305
Gustavian tables, screens, table lamps and MDF furniture.

Young and D Ltd.
Beckhaven House
9 Gilbert Road
London SE11 5AA
Tel: 0171-739 0537
Metal tables, taverna chairs.

Index

Acrylic goldsize, 16
Acrylic medium, 15
Acrylic paint, 10
Acrylic primer, 10, 20
    testing, 44
Acrylic scumble, 15
Ageing
    after painting, 26
    antiquing glaze, with, 26
    before painting, 25
    coloured waxes, with, 26
    two-part crackle varnish, with, 26
Antiqued kitchen cupboard, 30–33
Antiquing glaze, 26
Applying paint, 24
Artist's brushes, 12

Bathroom cabinet, découpaged, 43–46
Bedside chest, stencilled, 62–65, 89
Betrothal chests, painted, 47
Blanket box, handprinted, 47–50, 90
Bronzing powder, 16
Brushes, 12
Butler's tray, lacquered, 78–82, 91, 92
Buying furniture, 6

Chairs
    chequered, 51–54
    crackle-glazed, 37–39
Chequered table and chair, 51–54
Chests
    bedside, stencilled, 62–65, 89
    handpainted, 40–42, 88
Clear waxes, 13
Clock cupboard, lined, 75–77

Coloured waxes, 14
    ageing with, 26
Colours
    choosing, 21
    complementary, 21, 22
    mixing, 21, 22
    natural earth pigments, 21
    palette, 24
Crackle glaze, 15
Crackle-glazed chair, 37–39
Crackle varnish
    sealing, 27
    two-part, 14, 26
Craquelure lamp base, 58–61
Cupboard
    antiqued kitchen, 30–33
    lined clock, 75–77
Cutting equipment, 17
Cutting mat, 17

Découpage, 6
    technique, 43
Découpaged bathroom cabinet, 43–46
Designs, ideas for, 25
Distressing surface, 26
Dragged effect, 55
Drawing instruments, 17

Emulsion paint, 10

Fillers, 16
Fine pointed brushes, 12
Finishing
    crackle varnish, after applying, 27
    matt finish, 27
    satin finish, 27
    waxed finish, 27
Finishing paper, 13
Flat-haired synthetic brushes, 12

Frame
mirror, gilded, 66–70
picture, limed, 34–36
Frottage technique, 83
Frottaged and stencilled screen, 83–87, 93
Furniture waxes, 13, 14

Gilded mirror frame, 66–70
Gilding, 66, 68
Gilt creams, 17
Glazes, 15
Glues, 16
Goldsize, acrylic, 16

Handpainted chest, 40–42, 88
Handprinted blanket box, 47–50, 90
Harlequin theme, 51
Hog fitches, 12
Household paint brushes, 12

Kitchen cupboard, antiqued, 30–33

Lacquered butler's tray, 78–82, 91, 92
Lacquer technique, 80
Lacquerwork, 6
Lamp base, craquelure, 58–61
Limed picture frame, 34–36
Liming, 34
Liming wax, 14
Lined clock cupboard, 75–77

Manicure scissors, 17
Masking tape, 17
Matt finish, 27
Medium density fibreboard (MDF), 6, 20
Mediums, 15
Metal leaf, 16

Metal, preparing, 20
Metal table, verdigris, 71–74, 91
Methylated spirit, 16
Mirror frame, gilded, 66–70
Mouldings, 66
Mutton cloth, 17

Natural earth pigments, 21

Oil-based primer, 10
Oil-based varnish, 15
Oriental lacquerwork, 78

Paint, 10
stencilling, for, 64
Painted betrothal chests, 47
Painting
applying paint, 24
colours, choosing, 21
handpainted chest, 40–42, 88
mixing colours, 21, 22
pigment and paint, mixing, 22
Paper
glue, 16
tracing paper, 17
transfer paper, 17
Parchment shade, sealing, 61
Pattern, surface, 24
Picture frame, limed, 34–36
Powdered pigments, 10
paint and paint mediums, mixing with, 22
Preparation, 20
Primers, 10, 12
PVA medium, 15

Rottenstone, 10
Ruler, 17
Rust-inhibiting primer, 12

Sandpaper, 13

Satin finish, 27
Scalpel knife, 17
Scandinavian painted furniture, 55
Screen, frottaged and stencilled, 83–87, 93
Scumble, acrylic, 15
Scumble-glazed table, 55–57
Set square, 17
Shellac, 6, 14, 20
Soft-haired mops, 12
Solvents, 16
Specialist decorating brushes, 12
Stencil brushes, 12
Stencil film, 17
Stencilling
bedside chest, 62–65, 89
designs, 62
frottaged screen, 83–87, 93
handprinted blanket box, 47–50, 90
paint for, 64
Stencil making, 17
Straight edge, 17
Surface patterns, 24
Sword liners, 12, 75, 76

Table
chequered, 51–54
scumble-glazed, 55–57
verdigris metal, 71–74, 91
Templates
frottaged and stencilled screen, 93
handpainted chest, 88
handprinted blanket box, 90
lacquered butler's tray, 91, 92
stencilled bedside chest, 89
verdigris metal table, 91
Three-panelled screen, 83

Tracing paper, 17
Traditional paint, 10
Transfer metal leaf, 16
Transfer paper, 17
Tray
butler's, lacquered, 78–82, 91, 92
Two-part crackle varnish, 14
ageing with, 26

Varnish brushes, 12
Varnishes, 14, 15
Verdigris metal table, 71–74, 91

Water-based products, 6
Water-based varnish, 14
Water-soluble pencil, 17
Waxed finish, 27
Wax resist, 30, 32
Waxes, 13, 14
Whiteboard
painting, 43
preparing, 20
White spirit, 16
Wire brushes, 13
Wire wool, 13
Wood filler, 16
Wood glue, 16
Wood, preparing, 20

ACKNOWLEDGEMENTS

Thanks to Sally Winter of 78 Southwick Road, Bournemouth BH6 6PV, for supplying the beautiful etching of shells I have used in the limed picture frame.

I would also like to thank my husband for his enormous help and support, my family for putting up with the general chaos and lack of space while I was painting the furniture, and Elaine Green for her encouragement and support.

The following companies kindly loaned props for photography:

Antiques and Things (tel: 0171-350 0597) supplied a lace napkin and antique china; **Cologne & Cotton** (tel: 0171-736 9261) supplied bed linen, slippers, a nightdress and cologne; **Bella Figura at Rogers & Co** (tel: 0171-731 8504) supplied gilt sconces; **Hamleys** (tel: 0171-287 0562) supplied wooden toys, coloured pencils and a hobby horse; **Jerrys Home Store** (tel: 0171-581 0909) supplied white china, a blue and white napkin, blue and white china, an apple basket, face cloths and a wooden nail brush; **Rita Martinez** (tel: 0171-731 8617) supplied old flower pots; and **Robson Watley International** (tel: 0181-466 0830) supplied dried flowers.
Dover Publications supplied the alphabet on p.90